Kayakmen

Tales of Greenland's Seal Hunters

Collected by Signe Rink
Translated by Torben Hutchings

Adventures in New Lands: Volume 10

Other titles in this series

Originally published as
*Kajakmaend, Fortaellinger af
Gronlandske Saelhundefangere*
Copenhagen, 1896

Funded in part by
DANISH ARTS FOUNDATION
Copenhgen, Denmark

First English edition
copyright 2016 IPI Press

Design: IPI Press

ISBN 978-0-9961938-4-9

✦

International Polar Institute Press
Post Office Box 212
Hanover, New Hampshire 03755 USA

Kayakmen

Tales of Greenland's Seal Hunters

Collected by
Signe Rink

Translated by Torben Hutchings

Distributed by University Press of New England
upne.com

Contents

Preface

Around the years 1850-60, Greenlanders practically owned no other reading material beyond their religious books, hymn books, the Testaments and some exemplary short stories, occasionally collected and translated by zealous priests, such as Fabricius, Kragh, Kjær senior, Vandal, Optatus Steenberg and more, but these books could in no way be classified as entertainment reading.

In the meanwhile there gradually arose—and in particular around the above years, although also somewhat earlier—a number of good textbooks from the country's younger priests, among which particular mention should go to (partly as independent authors, partly as contributors) the pastors Carl Janssen, H. Jørgensen, Kjær junior as well as the Herrnhut missionary S. Kleinschmidt. These texts again concerned the school and the "Seminary," the institute of higher education at Godthaab for the education of younger Catechists. The only popular reading, so to speak, had until then been solely comprised of a rather peculiar collection of writings, namely: Wieland's

Oberon, Ingemann's Holger *Danske* as well as his *Voice in the Desert,* translated into Greenlandic by pastor P. Kragh. These articles only existed as manuscripts, which were in such demand that, for a number of years, they were circulated from house to house and from colony to colony, until they finally could neither be read, nor remain in one piece any more. The undersigned has both seen and read from several of these unravelling, age-yellowed manuscripts. Futhermore, during the translator's childhood there existed a—one might think rather thoughtlessly compiled—book of ballads, which began with "The dove grows on our globe" and finished with, "My son, if you want to advance in the world, then bow!"

This collection also brought joy, although the greatest contributors were probably the appealing tunes and the translator's luck with rhymes and rhythms, something the locals had quite an ear for, but which they had mostly gone without in the translation of the older psalms.

In addition to what is mentioned here, the Greenlanders also gained reliable social entertainment from their legends, as inherited from time immemorial; even among these fairytale legends, of which there were hundreds, they liked to single out examples of the most popular ones for transcription and mutual lending.

This, combined with their desire for the translations brought to them from outside, unequivocally showed that the present Greenlanders had a certain literary craving, and 1861, with this view of the conditions, the first printing house in Greenland was established—the same one to which this book owes its origination. At the same time as the printing house was established, an invitation went out to the natives, near and far, to provide contributions to a journal with biographies and accounts of journeys, hunting incidents and stories generally of any type and nature.

The idea for this was conceived by the translators now late husband, then Inspector of South Greenland, Dr. H. Rink, later director of the Royal Greenlandic Trade in Copenhagen. He was strongly supported by the Doctor at Godthaab, Dr. Th. Lindorff, as well as by the principle of the seminary H. Jørgensen and Missionary Kleinschmidt. The directorate in the motherland also readily gave its consent to carry the costs, just as the endeavor was later led, in a most understanding way, by Rink's successors to the office: Inspectors Stephensen and Ryberg.

The plan was to use the funds flowing in to create an annual booklet, which was to be printed over the course of the winter and be ready for when the shipping routes between the colonies opened up again at the start of the summer. It succeeded in this completely, and *Atuagagdliutit*—the title of the new entertainment periodical—is still, after 40 years of existence, fully viable. It is edited, illustrated, printed, bound and shipped all by one man, the native Lars Møller (Arkaluk), whose name has often enough been mentioned in all kinds of accounts from Greenland, both domestic and foreign.

The booklet is distributed for free through each colony administration, which received a certain number of copies each year to be distributed to the respective districts. In return, new voluntary contributions flow in from all edges of the country, and there are few of these that don't begin with: "Since it is so incredibly entertaining to read *Atuagagdliutit*, I too will now also provide my contribution," as well as other similar expressions.

It is from these, somewhat broadly presented but otherwise interesting, contributions and depictions, that the undersigned has made a selection, partially in the conviction that they might gain readers among the audience, and partially from a cultural historic purpose, in as much as that there is hereby provided the first and only presentation of independent Greenlandic, or indeed Eskimoic, literature that has ever appeared in the world. The great collection of the historic legends of the past are—though indeed recounted by Greenlanders—all written down, published and partially adapted by Europeans, whereas the present text, as mentioned, through its entire process of creation, comprises a first-hand account, through which the civilized modern Greenlander provides a true picture of himself and his age, while his heathen ancestors have managed to pass along orally.

The authors of "Kayakmen" are, in spite of their many true European names, no less all true Greenlanders—we deliberately don't say true Eskimos, since, as is well known, the part of this tribe living in Greenland is now very mixed.

There is a very noticeable difference between the narrative skills of our native authors, as some understand how to organize both materials and thoughts most sensibly, while others—to the translator's infinite bother—throw things in helter-skelter. As far as the present selection concerns, the author's personality stands out quite clearly, in spite of the somewhat learned narrative style of the modern age: with Petrus Lynge it is touching naiveté and good-natured satire; with Ungâralak the superiority of the conventional kayak-man; with Aparâvigssuak convivial craftiness (hence in part his name, or rather the connection to the latter).

My original favorite idea: to provide a completely literal translation, soon had to be abandoned for various reasons—mainly due to being far too preventative of even moderately pleasant reading, but I have otherwise kept as close to the style of the original insofar as the Greenlandic is compatible with the Danish. It has here and there been necessary to add a word or a parenthesis in order to explain the far too unknown situations or conditions, in particular because our authors, who wrote for their own countrymen, whom they pretty much knew themselves to have an understanding of in advance, often only provided partial information for.

As far as the completely literal translation concerns, such a thing would roughly end up sounding like this: "Daniel, that time he didn't want to carry the mail for the administrator, but because he in the same instance could visit him other (who lived there) whereto the administrator planned to send mail— then he began to want to anyway, and reversed from his first inclination, he then carried the mail for the administrator anyway, even though he initially didn't want to."

It has also in certain cases been tempting to cut out things as being too repetitive, and particularly among them a certain types of tiresome, plagiaristic reflections, wherein Greenlanders generally, but perhaps particularly the catechists, seem to gain pleasure from writing.

On yet another point I don't resist anticipating the reader's judgement or providing them with a bit of a clue. For the reader may potentially wonder that the present tales arouse so little excitement, though they contain such powerful sensational material as; umiaks and kayaks sinking before the narrator's eyes; kayak-men, with no hope of rescue, sitting down to freeze to death on drifting ice floes in the middle of the wild sea; that a despairing child drowns themself; and that scores of people that have starved to death are found clustered beneath the ruins of their houses ... What effects could such subjects not conjure up if given European treatment! But the Greenlander thinks very little of wanting to "affect," he simply wants to clearly explain what it is he, or someone else, has experienced; and secondly, circumstances force him, in a way, to view the wondrous in an everyday light, for every moment of his existence as a kayak-man, the same things that he has recounted of someone else might become his own lot, and he must display equanimity towards it, even the great things. It is entirely another case when the narrator, still freshly filled by the wondrous or the ghastly, verbally recounts it—either on his own or on his friends behalf—for in such a case his tale is accompanied by the most unrivaled mimicry and a wealth of vivid expressions, which only slightly match the talent of his pen.

And I hereby surrender, to the honored public, a work that I, in spite of much serious diligence, do not dare consider flawless.

Signe Rink
Kristiania, November 1895

Kayakmen

A Fishing Trip
by
Kristoffer Nielsen

∎

For a long while we had not been able to
go out in our kayaks due to bad weather and
thin ice, but on the 21st of February things had
cleared sufficiently that some of us decided to
row across and go fishing at Angpalartok; 'us' being myself, my brother Kali, Daniel and Ungak.
When we left a steady easterly wind was blowing. We had hardly started before it began to
pick up. We resigned ourselves to it in the hope
that it wouldn't get any worse than it was, and
that we should be able to risk continuing. But
we had barely started fishing before snow began
to flurry from the peaks of all the fells around us,
and white-tops began to show on the sea—so
we immediately had to seek the shelter of the
land in order to bundle our fish together, and
then head home urgently. I had wanted to turn
around even before we had started fishing, but
Ungak would not hear of it.

For a moment it seemed as if the wind
would quiet, as it became more southerly, but
it only picked up again. Setting off across the
bay was now out of the question. Instead we
carefully kept to the shore. At Ekallunguit the
storm squalled so strongly that against our will,

we were carried out anyway, and it was all we could manage to make it over to Nunakarfigssuak. Here my brother wanted us to immediately seek the shore, but I suggested that we should instead try to get around the headland first. We may have been better off doing the former as the only thing we gained in doing so was a bit of shelter beneath the ice edge (without the option of getting ashore). We were, time and again, thrown out, and we were frozen half to death. My bundle of fish refused to stay on the kayak, and reluctant though I was, I had to let it go; something the others had me do much earlier. At that moment I heard a cry for help from nearby. It was my younger brother, who had lost control of his kayak and was drifting. I got a hold of him and set him right, but lost sight of him at the same moment, as we could see no further than an oar-length away in the flurrying snow. I now decided to try and beach myself with the surf, but an inconvenient iceberg was wedged in the only place where this was possible—frozen together with the ice edge itself. I had to squeeze my way past this iceberg. It was so impossible that I was instead thrown straight against it, and then thrown back again, until I finally had the luck to float past it and straight in, where at the decisive moment, I managed to throw my arms around a pointy rock, which poked out of the ice edge, and gained a hold.

I remained for a short while, until I could properly set my mind to climbing out of the kayak. When I finally did get ashore, I immediately started to inspect my ruined kayak, the keel of which had snapped in several places as a result of hard impacts against the iceberg. As I was doing this, I spotted Ungak through the snow and sea spray. He lay capsized quite near to me. I immediately let go of my own kayak and rushed to his aid. Getting a hold of him was very difficult, as he had fallen out of his kayak, but I finally managed to grab him and pull him up. He was surprisingly no worse off than he could immediately get up on his own and start brushing the water from his clothes, so I immediately asked him to look after himself, and then proceeded to look around.

And what did I see other than my own poor brother, hanging over the edge of his kayak like a dead man. I was practically paralyzed by this, but I gathered all my strength to help, as he lay there sloshing in the surf. In the end I managed to get a hold of him, pull him in and get to work on resuscitating him. As soon as he began to breathe again and came to his senses, I explained the necessity of quickly reaching the ruins (on the other side of the headland), and I now felt somewhat envious of Ungak, whom I had seen running off unaided because I had to both support Kali and carry him on my back, seeing he had almost no strength left. Unfortunately it was a bad, tiring snow that we had to wade through to get there, and Kali would both lurch and fall each time I let him walk on his own. In the end we did manage to reach the house, where the others went about sorting him out with straw from the ruin, so things didn't look too bad at all.

I now also set myself to tearing up straw and then kicked the hallway sufficiently clear of snow so that I could make a resting place for them, then all three of us sat down. If I exclude my kamiks, which had kept themselves dry until now, I was just as drenched as they were.

As we sat there, close against each other in the flurrying snow, which contributed a lot to our soaked state, I soon discovered that Ungak was anxiously starting to lose his color, and it was not long before he froze to death. He was so miserably clad!

His bare knees, as well as other limbs, could be seen everywhere through the holes in his poor clothes. I know nothing of what had become of him—he had not spoken.

My dear brother lived for a good while longer, and he would surely have made it through everything just fine had he only been able to change his clothes. By the time the tide dropped, he also began to display the signs, and as I had now grown certain that he was going to die, I spoke to him about the hereafter, so that he might prepare himself, as I was concerned for his soul. He had belonged to the more carefree and indifferent type. But he answered that I should not worry for him, for he held no fear, and he knew Jesus Christ and knew that he was the only savior. A great burden was lifted from my mind, and after that I only spoke of the bliss that he was soon to encounter in the homes of the blessed. In the end I sensed that he no longer heard me, and then I simply sat still next to him and saw how he faded further and further away. Then he sought out my eyes once more and, as he smiled to me, he expired. I was glad of the peace that I knew he felt in his final hour.

When I had arranged them somewhat, I went over the place from which one could look across to our settlement (on the other side of the water) in the hope that I might be spotted during a lull of the whirling snow, as I could assume that people were looking for us as best they could. I had indeed been seen, but of course couldn't be sure. I now once more returned to the dead and began to try to wring water out of my clothes, but each time I lifted the furs away from the heat of my body, they immediately froze. I would now have liked to have been able to set off across, but all three kayaks had been lost. It was, however, too sorrowful to sit next to the bodies, so I made my way over to one of the other plots to bide my time there. On the way I heard a voice speaking to me from the seaward side. It took me a good while, however, before I found my way down to the shouter, as my vision had been damaged in the terrible weather, so everything shone red and blue before my eyes. It was Nukagpiarak, who came with dry clothes; I must have been seen.

Since it was too difficult to get the clothes from him while keeping them dry, I preferred that he hurry back again to get me some means of transport. Of Daniel, who had come with us that morning, he said that he had got home alive, but without any skin on his face.

While I drifted around the water's edge waiting, I first bumped into my smashed kayak, and then Ungak's, but didn't touch it.[1] On the way across the sound I dreaded terribly the messages that I would now have to give to our poor relatives. The next day we brought the dead back in umiaks in calm weather.

1. According to ancient custom one should ideally not touch the property of the dead, let alone gain benefit from them. However, no rule without exception. Present distress thus sometimes breaks the old law or superstitious fear.

Hunting Adventure
by
Aparavigssuak

∎

Once, a long time ago, we were on a caribou hunt deep within the Godthaab fjord. We went across Tasserssuak (an inland lake, a good way from the fjord-bank) and set up camp by Majorkak's tent site, from which the Enok of Narsok and I ventured deeper inland to hunt. We didn't stop until we reached Kugssuak, the great river that flows from the inland ice. Here Enok immediately felled an animal, while we simultaneously, on one of the tips of land that jut out of the inland ice, spotted three more fully grown males. This was on the other side of the great river, and my friend didn't have the courage to cross it, which I felt the desire to attempt, especially as it was early in the morning (where the rivers, prior to the sun's effect on the ice, are not yet as full as they are later in the day). Besides, I only had myself to take care of, as the only thing I needed to carry was my rifle. I got across well enough, and just as I landed I immediately spotted two of the animals, which I shot right away. It didn't take long before I downed the third one. Immediately I began to flay it, as I saw the prime condition it was in, then I did the same with the two others. I peeled off the tallow and took out the stomachs, but this work was not quick. The sun was already quite high in the sky when I had to start thinking about returning over the river, and as mentioned, the rivers from the inland ice are not quite so easy to deal with. This ice had grown considerably since I last crossed it. Also, I had to carry a considerable burden around my neck. I packed the tallow and the stomachs and as much of the meat as possible to take with me in the skins of the three animals.[2]

I could see smoke from the hunter on the other side. Presumably he had lit a heather fire in order to keep the mosquitoes at bay, so I waded out with my heavy, unwieldy burden. I hadn't got far before I lost my boots, which had hung over the barrel of my gun. Worse was when the gun itself, which I carried on a strap, also slipped off my shoulder and fell in the river, where I had to lie on my knees on a rock and grasp after it. The water was clayey and cloudy, as is so often the case with all river water in the vicinity of the inland ice. I found it in the end, however, but I had to go a considerable distance down the river in order to catch my bundle of meat, which had luckily snagged on a rocky outcrop. It was only with great difficulty that I managed to get it up on my back again, before moving on. It now grew harder and harder to stay upright. As I

2. *The contents of the stomachs are considered delicacies.*

moved towards the middle of the river, the current grew stronger and deeper, so in the end I had water up to my waist with the bundle floating behind me, as the water helped buoy it. I fell again and had a harder time getting up than I did the first time; the increasing water masses grew stronger and stronger. I had the greatest difficulty locating the rifle, which this time, similarly to the last, fell to the bottom, since the place where it had sunk was not visible due to the rushing water out in the middle. I also had to venture quite a distance downstream in order to locate the skin bundle.

I did notice the anxiety that had come over the other hunter, as he ran back and forth along the river bank, and understood that it was out of concern for what might happen to me. Nonetheless he still got to see me fall once more, and this time was worse again.

I was on the last half of the river's width. Things were seriously bad this time, as my legs had gradually grown almost numb from the ice cold water, and I now really began to doubt whether I would manage to get up again. After several failed attempts I managed to, but couldn't muster the strength to get my burden up over my neck again, and I just let it drag behind me as best I could. In this way I finally reached shore, but Enok did say, wonderingly, that I had spent a worryingly long time under water, especially the last time. It was strange how large and strong the river had become!

The hunter quickly made another fire in

order to dry my wet clothes, while I ran around to keep some warmth in my body. Next he gave me the furry lining of his skin boots, as he made do with the outer boot. Without anything on my legs I would not have managed the rather long distance home to the tent by the freshwater lake, to which we only arrived late in the night.

The next day we went back and collected my prey. Before we started on our way back, I had the bearers press the water out of the skins and place everything out to dry, and I had them do this every time we made a longer stop on the journey. During one of these stops, one of them—it was Elias—wanted to make a detour by himself to see if he couldn't also catch himself a reindeer. After awhile he comes back instead of with a living animal, with his hands full of pieces given to him—cooked reindeer meat. There were thus other reindeer hunters not far away, without us being aware of it in the slightest, and to think these hunters had come from as far away as the Sugar loaf![3]

Nikolai from Agpat *(Greenlandic site near Godthaab)* must be able to recall these people, as he (according to them) once accompanied them

3. *The Sugar Loaf is a community in Greenland, so named for the shape of the mountains adjacent to it. This exclamation of astonishment speaks volumes about how stationary the Greenlandic Eskimos have become compared to past times, where summer journeys measuring hundreds of miles up and down the coast were not unusual. The distance in question here between the two colonies is about 25 miles.*

on a longer hunting trip. Of those that were part of the Sugar Loafer company, most are now dead, and of us Godthaabers, who went along, Enok and I are probably the only ones left. The trip, wherein the river nearly dragged me along with it, took place in 1854.

Later, in the year 1861, when I once "wintered" at Kornok *(trading post south of Godthab)*, it came to my attention that the Umanakks wanted to travel by boat up the Kangersunek river. I rowed there too, with a mind to join them on the trip. Just as I was about to turn into this branch of the fjord, without yet having seen any sign of umiak or kayaks, I spotted a Harbor seal amusing itself by jumping up and down from a smaller iceberg, before it eventually settled on top of it.

I rowed out to hurl my harpoon after it, but it had now crept so far in over the edge that I couldn't get close enough to it. I had to decide to shoot it (instead of catching it with a harpoon and bladder). Since at the time it was not as common to shoot from the kayak itself, as it later became, I had to disembark onto a little ice mound that lay a reasonably suitable distance from the iceberg with the seal on it and since the icy knoll only had space enough for me, I had to make do with placing my kayak as close against it as possible, then I prepared to shoot. Luckily I then looked down at the kayak, which was already beginning to drift away. I quickly brought it to again, and then I had to get serious about shooting. I did so and hit it right away.Now the kayak had drifted so far out that it was all I could do to reach the kayak paddle lying across it. In so doing I achieved nothing more than moving the oar out of place, by which it would most likely fall off and be lost. There I now stood, alone, on the little ice mound in the middle of the wide sound, staring at my kayak. It was still no further away than that I, by throwing myself into the sea, would have been able to reach it, but I lacked courage. Only when my infants and the others, for whom I was provider, realized that I would perish where I was, did I grasp my determination to leap out. Then I simply looked down at the water, and the feeling returned again, as if a sharp point of a knife was turned towards me. Only after I had made three failed run-ups, as I had second thoughts each time, did I finally throw myself out. Once I was out, the coolness of the water refreshed and enlivened me in such a way that I no longer thought it that bad.

I also managed to get a hold of the kayak quite quickly. In my confusion I grabbed it (too quickly) right by the hole, accidentally capsizing it. When I clung to its upturned bottom with both arms, I ended up spinning it all the way around, after which I finally managed to get it upright again. Now it was both full of water and the skin was quite soaked, so there now seemed to be little else of it above water than the pointed bows. I quickly tore loose the hunting bladder to keep myself afloat, and with this in one hand, I crept along the side of the kayak to the stern, which I slowly and carefully pressed down far enough for me to climb over it, and from there, astride it, crept over to the middle and sat there in the hole. As I sank into it, I felt as if I was about to sink to the bottom. Sitting there, holding the bladder, which lay in the sea outside the kayak, I sat with the water almost up to my mouth. By pulling the bladder further forward, I felt it rise somewhat, for which reason I now attempted to leash it to the front straps *(taqqaq)*, which wasn't easy to do under water (I managed, however). Now the kayak really tilted backwards, however I considered it a considerable advantage that, through this, I got my whole head above water. The oar—which, by the way, I had so far not even considered—hung (against all expectations) along the kayak side, remarkably tangled in the hunting line, so I could now, slowly and carefully, start rowing under water. It took a tremendously long time to simply reach Tigunertak. Once I was there, I thought that I would easily get out and sort myself out. First getting the water poured out of the kayak, then getting myself warmed up. When I finally got across, my lower body was so stiff that I could only manage to creep to begin with. In this way I reached a stone, to which I fastened the kayak.

Now I attempted to get up, but fell over every time–many times! In the end I managed to right myself, more or less, and turned the kayak upside down so the water could run out, and rowed (in a normal way) back to the ice mound to collect my gun, which I had left there. When I turned to look back, my vision failed completely, so all the large fells about me vanished completely from sight. The same had, by the way, happened to me on the trip to Tigunertak when I was rowing with my arms under water and only had my head free. However, I soon reached the ruin on Nunaruluk,[4] just across from Ivnajuatok, where it went no better than at Tigunertak. Here, for the time being, I also had to settle for fastening my kayak to a rock instead of bringing it ashore. I did manage to regain my strength somewhat, as there was so much straw on the ruin that I could, several times, replace the layer with which I padded myself beneath my wet clothes. In the end I was well enough at ease that I could haul the kayak up, and even later in the afternoon I could row across to the iceberg that bore my slain seal, from which I immediately extracted the liver, and ate on the spot, along with some of the belly fat. After this last excursion I prepared to overnight in the ruin.

While I sat there, the Iserssarnak *("the wind, when it blows in")* began to really blow. If I had been out on the ice mound, I'd soon have been done for. Some time into the next day I made it back to Kornok, without having seen the slightest of the umiak that I had originally set out because of. As it later turned out, I had mistaken

4. *The term "Ruin" is generally understood as wall-remnants from Greenland's first discoverers "the Norse"; for walls left by the Eskimos or Greenlanders, the term "house-remnant" will be used.*

the date of the Umanakk's departure, so had seen nothing of them.

The iceberg, upon which there was blood from the seal, they had spotted on a later journey, but one could never have guessed that I had any part of it being bloodied.

A good catch.

A Dangerous Mail Journey Over the Ice
By
Casper Nielsen

∎

I, writing this, am catechist Casper Nielsen from the Disko fjord.

It is now many years since the following occurred, but as I am perpetually encouraged by my countryman Gerhard Kleist, I must, although I feel rather inept at it, to the best ability of my memory, narrate my wanderings and my sufferings in the great, lonely expanses *(inuilarssuarme)*.

In January, ice mail arrived from Egedesminde to Kronprinzens Island, where I lived at the time. The mail was for the Inspector at Godhavn, but the postmen did not want to go any further than this,[5] because my uncle and I were chosen to take the mail onwards.

I was 20 years old at the time, and my mother scolded me for having agreed; she probably thought I didn't need the money. Kronprinzens Island was at that time rich in seals, and she would rather not go without wanting to miss out on the catches. The decision had been made, and we had to go as soon as the weather cleared a bit. This occurred on the 24th of January.

5. *A distance of 4 miles.*

When we set off at dawn, the Disko Island, which we were to journey to, was completely hidden from us in the fog. Who would have thought that we wouldn't make it there over the course of the day, instead of ending up spending the night on the ice in great misery? We had got lost in the fog, constantly round and round, utterly blind. Towards evening we finally encountered some footprints, which headed outwards at first, but later seemed to be heading back towards land again. I suggested following these, but since I could not convince my uncle, I let him have his way—we turned back. After wandering for some time we passed an iceberg that had frozen fast, which we immediately recognized as having passed once before, and when we soon managed to reach the *stamukhi*,[6] he decided to spend the night there, and I did the same. It was cold, but calm enough that it might do. Later in the night a storm came with ice-mist and fog. The condition we ended up in as a result became my first proper test of kayaking life, but worse things were to come.

With the break of day there was no change. We didn't despair because there was otherwise nothing wrong with us, so my uncle once more set a course for Godhavn. I was not satisfied with his decision this time either, knowing how violently the northern wind

6. *Screw-ice. The ice, crushed by waves and the current, builds itself piece-by-piece into walls and ramparts, which in an emergency may provide some shelter in the white desert.*

tended to blow, with gusts down across Ka-rusuk's leeward side. I insisted that we should rather go home again; we had once during a clearing of the weather been able to spot and note the iceberg of our home region . . . but he didn't want to do this. We always know little of what awaits us, and we can only bow to God's will in all things.

So we fought our way forwards against the storm with our kayaks on our head; Dinas in front and myself angry and sullen behind. Several times I fell into cracks, hidden by more fresh snow, somehow not getting wet. We walked all day again. As night fell, my uncle had gone snow blind.

Here in the middle of the ice in the biting storm, and equally far from shore in both directions, there was little hope of rescue. We once more spent the night on the ice, without knowing where we were. During a slight morning clearing I immediately understood that we must be almost directly off the colony (though far from the coast). I wanted to hurry as best I could to reach it. I asked Dinas to stay calmly where he was, but turned often to look for him and soon saw the poor thing come staggering after me with the kayak on his head, always mis-stepping and wobbling in the most rugged ice. Without a second thought I threw down my kayak and ran back to carry his for him. Leading him by the hand we finally reached my starting point, where we once more had to carry our own kayaks, and we wandered for the entirety of the day in this way. Only later in the evening did I discover, south of Kitdlit *("a gap in the ice")* which by its direction seemed that it must reach land.

I now gained new hope that I might possibly get him back by following this crack along the leeward side of a row of grounded icebergs. Nothing was to come of this though. I lashed our kayaks together as well as could be done, in order to bring the blind man with me. We had not gone far before the sea came barreling into us and, to my horror, began to break the ice into bits around us, hurling us backwards and forwards between the ice floes, greatly fearful of having our kayaks smashed to bits. My only wish now was simply to get up on the solid ice again. I, who still had my sight, could probably avoid being squeezed or torn to shreds, but my companion could not possibly manage, and I could see how his kayak gradually settled lower and lower into the water.

He would not have said anything of his own accord, but when I finally asked him, he admitted that he was sitting in water and felt wet. As I had to consider his rescue abandoned, I felt that it was always more pleasant to row with the wind at one's back rather than in one's face, and once more turned from land. For awhile we simply rowed about randomly, until I finally discovered a medium-large ice floe with a small pile of snow on it. The ice piece lay wallowing back and forth, rocking up and down, and I took advantage of the moment it drifted in to shoot him up onto it. I succeeded, after which I made as good a seat for him as was possible. As soon as I managed to place him there, he asked that I should please let him stay where he was and think only of myself. I wouldn't do that while there was still nothing wrong with him.[7] In that case I could be viewed as being complicit in his death; and it was only late into the night that I could resolve myself to leave him. Then he asked me to sing a psalm over him, but contrary to my conviction, I answered that there was still nothing wrong with him, and that, were I to sing over him, it would look as is I wished for his death. He, the poor thing, also told me that he suffered pangs of conscience, as he had left his wife for another in youth.

When I had finally left him, I set my course directly for land, across bad ice and spent the rest of the night seated in my kayak on the ice, some way east of him. When the morning broke, I sought to establish where I was. Unfortunately I saw enough to establish this: here I sat directly off the promontory they call Uivfat *(The Ferns)*—the one that forms the curve of the Disko fjord. I now considered myself hopelessly lost, and since I knew no better, turned to the heavens and prayed: "I know I am sinful, but I beg you anyway, Almighty Father, that my body,

7. *Meaning: so long as the symptoms of freezing to death have not occurred. When there is no longer any hope of survival, the Greenlanders no longer consider it wrong to leave the person in distress in order to save themselves.*

once my soul has departed, may find its rest on land, rather than on the bottom of the sea, so those left behind may thus understand that we truly perished."[8] I still sat immovable and perplexed when the ice beneath me suddenly cracked, immediately sinking down with the kayak. The crack also led towards land, but I did not move from where I was, not before the gap had expanded enough for me to row freely.

Now I had to start rowing. I seriously missed my kayak gloves. I had let him keep them, though I probably knew that he wouldn't need them for much longer. For two days without stop I rowed in this crack, without leaving the kayak so much as once, and had so far avoided having my hands freeze. While I remained within the widened crack—as close as possible to the landward side, so as not to risk drifting out to sea—it grew quite quiet. As I rowed, I saw the sea with many snow-covered ice floes, a sight that immediately made me immensely thirsty.

When it finally grew light, I heard a rumbling sound from the north, which (I later understood) had been the ice-calving in the Disko fjord, and when I reached open sea, the kayak picked up a mighty speed, up and down, as a storm was blowing, flurries falling from the high fells. It was no longer possible for me to keep the backs of my

8. *This refers to the superstition that kayak men that suffered misadventure, or any person that suffers misadventure, whose corpse does not appear, are seen as kivigtut—people who have deliberately fled society and are feared to be ghosts.*

hands free of frost, so my only recourse was to constantly dip them as deeply in the sea as possible on each oar-stroke. When this wouldn't do in the long run, I had to pull a lacing strap out of my kayak clothes to wrap around them, and this helped wonderfully.

I wallowed mightily, ran up the waves and then down again, until I finally found a landing place far to the west. This was the lowland of the Disko fjord, but the ice edge towards the sea was so terribly high and difficult that, with my heavily iced-up kayak, I barely managed to get up onto it. By knocking off the ice as far forward as I could reach in my seated position, I finally managed to work my way up. This was during the light of mid-day. I quickly took my kayak over my head and sped along across the solid ground. I was, however, still in some doubt as to whether it was frozen sea or lowland that I was walking on, until I discovered a yellow straw poking out of the snow. So, God be praised, I had actually made it to land!

I soon found a cave where I could store my kayak, from which I first retrieved the letter pouch as well as a box and a little stone jar that I still wished to bring to its destination. Doubt arose as to which was the route I should take, and whether it should be south around the high fells or behind them. I chose behind, and would you believe it—it was right way!

To begin with I was quite at ease and had already made good headway by the time it grew dark again. I was quite scared and uneasy about the long, deep gully I knew I would have to go down through, but while the dark gathered closer and closer in around me when I finally reached it and wandered into it—nothing evil befell me.

As I later wandered across the open plains, I at once spotted, in the middle of the smooth snow, a massively big dog with droopy ears. When I reached it, it turned out just to be a stone, poking out of the snow. I walked around it a couple of times and then continued. Soon after I discovered two Greenlanders drilling, with their toqs *(round staff with an iron point or pick at the end)*, at an ice arch (of the kind that rivers and waterfalls like to form in frost). I thought it was two people drilling for water, and now a terrible thirst came over me once more. I began to run as best I could towards it. When I arrived there was nothing, neither ice arch nor people. I couldn't help but kick at the snow with my heels, but there was nothing to be found of what I thought I had seen.

I moved on and after some time entered deep snow with water beneath it. This was a nasty little wade in the dark; I didn't completely get away with it either, falling off a small incline somewhere, down into even more water, and lay fumbling for a long time until I got back on my feet. I was no longer short of drinking water though, and drank eagerly. When I began to freeze mightily, I quickly moved on. Finally I came down from the fells onto the ice. It had grown pitch dark, but I soon spotted three sleds that were driving past, then stopped a little way ahead of me. How happy I was! The thought struck me that it might again be one of my false visions . . . "Yes, are they Disko men," I thought, then they will probably address you—let's see!

As it happened, my senses had once more betrayed me, and regardless of the fact that I, right up until the end, could see both the driver standing ready to grab the sled's rear bar and the dogs ready to leap forwards. While I wandered forward in the dark, I at once heard a fine, small voice from above saying: "Now you're going too far east." I investigated the context, and as I drove the staff into the ice with my left hand, I turned right immediately, where I was met by a small flickering light in the middle of a little haze of fog.

The light was neither above or below my line of sight, but directly in front of it, and I walked straight forwards towards it. It was as if I was surrounded by an entire swarm of people, and it grew lighter and lighter in front of me. I was now down on the ice itself and walked alongside the land. When I came to a small slope, I had grown so tired that I twice simply wanted ed to be allowed to sleep for a short moment, but sleep didn't find me. When I sat down for the third time, I heard a noise from above, as if from wind instruments. I took this as a sign that I was not allowed to sit down to sleep here either. Then I walked again for a bit. As I came to the place that they called Kitdlit, and spotted the high fell above the Godhavn colony, the light vanished. At this point I immediately felt that my feet had frozen.

On the morning of the 28th of January I finally arrived in Godhavn, but had to crawl on all fours up the slippery hill that leads up to the inspector's residence from the ice. It was so early in the day that people hadn't got up yet.

I didn't go to the huts of my countrymen first, but straight in to the inspector's residence, where I luckily found the cook awake. He stood in the kitchen, but could not recognize me. He immediately gave me a piece of fat-bread, but it tasted like earth on my tongue. He forbade me to drink water and then went in to the inspector, who he said still lay asleep. However, he came straight out of bed when he heard that the food tasted like earth to me. He immediately took a cup full of wine, into which he poured something warming (rum or brandy), and said that I should just empty it. Perhaps it warmed me, but in the same moment I lost my strength completely. He forbade me to go into the warm. When I got up to try to walk, I could not move so much as one foot.

If God will let me live for a few more years, I will tell you something more of the time I became catechist out here at Disko fjord (Kangerdluk). For now, look at what little I have written down, and then live well all my fellow accomplices in the sins of the world.

My Pilot Trip With the Americans

by
David Danielsen—Seal hunter

█

Since it has now grown customary that we Greenlanders let various accounts be printed, and since it is very entertaining to read them, I would now also like to narrate something from my travel with the Americans.[9]

I remember that we noted the 16th of July and that we in no way expected a visit from any kind of vessel that day. It was rumored though that a foreign ship was heading up the fjord towards us. It soon turned out to be an American one, and that the occasion for its visit was to take me with it. My countryman, Nicolai from God-havn, was already on board, it was said. I thought I had to go along, when they asked me, so I took our catechist's kayak on loan. It was at sunset that I went on board. During the night we made it beyond the Upernivik colony, which we only passed around midday the next day.

9. *While the narrator mentions neither the name of the captain or the ship that came and took him on as a pilot and interpreter, or even hints at the purpose of the journey, it is obvious that what is referred to is Lieutenant Garlington's rescue expedition for Greely with the ship Proteus. According to the later Greely accounts, Proteus was crushed and sank beneath the ice in Smithsund on the 23rd of July 1883, almost directly out from Cape Isabella.*

The following morning we made it onto the Baffin ice. Here we encountered both floes and larger connected ice masses, until in the end, we were completely hemmed in by the ice. It was frightening to watch because of its running. Then we sailed and sailed and finally sighted the heathen site Gebior *(misunderstood pronunciation of Cape York)*. We reached there at twelve noon, but (unfortunately) found none of the eskimos at home. The ice pushed in on us in such a way that we couldn't leave before well into the night. When I next came on deck, I found us again anchored at a large island, where there was an upturned longboat, under which immense quantities of provisions and guns were stored.

Somewhere, not far from here, there was a shed similarly full of foodstuffs, and outside was left a small steamer. Due north we eventually, after we had once more sailed for awhile, come across several additional coal-bunkers, as large as entire beaches full of pebbles. We continued to find similar provision bunkers (depots left by previous travelers) for awhile.

Then we had to leave the eastern coast and set off across to the American side, where we went up onto the fells in a deep bay to see what the waters were like to the north. Since this revealed open water, we quickly had to leave again. It wasn't long before we reached the pack ice, and the Captain would have turned around again, but the ice drew in so quickly that we were completely surrounded by it in a moment. At 1 o'clock we were already so stuck that we were immediately lifted up and laid on our side in such a way that we had great difficulty in walking along the deck. The bulwarks fell and the helm splintered with a racket which made one's head sore. Now haste was made to haul supplies out onto the ice. This had to happen at such a speed that people even had to let the stern boats fall (there was no time to lower them). Thankfully only one of them was somewhat damaged. We Greenlanders were of course most eager to get our kayaks to safety out on the ice.

We were, more or less, saved!

It was wonderful to see the speed with which the ship sank. The yards snapped like twigs and vanished into the depths, and everything vanished from before our eyes in a moment. Then there was nothing left of the American ship other than what we had thrown out onto the ice. The first night after the sinking we stayed here during a massive storm. The next morning we began to bring the rescued items in to the coast (Cape Isabella). Once finished with this, we made ourselves a shelter by spreading a sail across a cleft. It was a wonderful feeling to be on solid ground again. We spent a whole two days here saving supplies in caves in the rock.[10]

Of course now we (unfortunately) once more had to go out across the great water. We

10. *These depots were found on the 8th of October by the Greely expedition traveling south, who were to meet their fatal winter of starvation relatively near where their rescue ship had sunk.*

could just glimpse the land there as a narrow strip across the horizon. After a good day's worth of sailing we made it there and landed at four o'clock in the morning at a place that was a good deal more northerly than Gebior. We had sailed before a good northern wind. As soon as we had rested sufficiently, we had to leave again, and the Americans predicted to my friend and I that we would probably end up with skinless hands. What did we care, that would be the least of our worries. Besides, we know that humans aren't created to live purely in plenty. It is necessary for us that we also experience adversity, and what is imposed on us by our lord we should suffer without grumbling. We sailed for yet another day before a strong wind, and slept the next night on the pebbles ashore and felt very exhausted. My friend wept from anxiety and forebodings. I asked him to stop doing so if he wanted any comfort from me. Were he to be reasonable, I would help him as much as I could.

The next night we pulled up the boats and slept on the ice. It was their the officers intent to seek possible passing ships around Gebior, for which reason we had to head there. One of our boats, the one I wasn't in, left a day ahead of the rest, but we caught up with it at the heathens at Gebior (this time they were there).

Customs were different here than with us in Greenland. Their maidens walked fully clad in Blue Fox skins, while all older women only used them for leg-wear, and wore seal skins on their upper body.

The men walked in bear skins, so everything was different to how it was with us in Greenland, but friendly they were.

After a five day stay, we prepared to go further south, and they relieved themselves of quite a number of provisions due to the expanse of water that we now had to tackle. The heathens were gifted many tin cans of meat. Once again it blew violently, and our boats were separated for a while as they each took the wind from a different side. We could sweep onwards in the dense fog without risking running into one another. I was now anything but comfortable, and could only pray to the master of the waves for my life, to the merciful God, who alone can preserve us.

The waves rose around us like mountains, and once they broke over the boat in such a way that it was as if we were immediately sinking deeply, an incident occurred that I simply cannot refrain from narrating.

As soon as they began to doubt their rescue, they all began to drink lots of brandy, and dearly wanted me to do so as well. Though I didn't want to for a long time, they eventually got me to join in, as the officer of our boat said that I ought to. After that point I joined in each time the others had some.

The officer asked if I thought we would be able to reach Disko. When I replied that I couldn't say, he said: "No, with this storm it is impossible." Eventually we had enough visibility for us to see land, but it quickly closed in again, so we once more sat wrapped in the dark of the fog. Once it cleared properly we viewed the most wonderful darkening land to the south, and now things became pleasant for myself and Nicolai, while with growing quiet, we set off through a belt of large and small ice, which we often had to pole out of the way of our bows. The ice came from an immensely large glacier ashore. We spent three days getting past it, and it was shining white with pure ice. We had not left the boats since Gebior, nor did we do so until we were a day's journey from Upernivik.

As we had thought, we reached there the day after this, our first landfall. At 1 o'clock the same day we travelled south to Kangerdlugssutsiaq, then spent 10 days to Disko, the land that I had almost given up hope of ever re-seeing. Here the others arrived just in time to encounter a ship for their return journey.

God be praised!

On Incidents Where
I Have Been Endangered
By
Karl Olrik

∎

Since I find the "entertainment periodical" so particularly amusing, I too wish to provide a couple of narrations of things that I have experienced since I began to move out and about.

At the start of my time as a kayakman, I could never get enough of being out, and was never afraid of anything. I enjoyed myself the most in proper swells.

One day, in a good south-westerly, my friend Anton Dalager and I dearly wanted to go out to practice, and we didn't resist our urge, even though the elders strongly advised us against it; they felt that we were not trained enough to expose ourselves to such seas. We dearly wanted to go. The kayak already began to take water across it. We thought this was outrageously entertaining, and said to each other: Let us row into the wind and see if we can stay on top of the waves? Ashore, Anton's father watched. After some time passed I gave up and turned out of the wind again, while my friend, on the other hand, endured. As I approached the fjord, I lost control of my kayak, and no matter how I strained and used the oar, one moment to the right, the other moment to the left, it did not help. I continued to drift, and during yet another attempt at back-paddling, I capsized. In my initial surprise I let go of the oar. I quickly got a hold of it again, then once more let it slip from my hands, with the thought that my friend would undoubtedly discover me. When I finally felt something fumbling near my shoulder while I was upside down in the water, I only had a vague understanding that someone must be near me, for I was, at this point, very close to asphyxiating and losing consciousness. I vaguely recall that I made an effort to help, by reaching up with my arms, but instead of grabbing a hold of my rescuer's kayak deck, which I thought I had done, I was later told that I had simply drummed on the bottom of his kayak.

After this I knew nothing until I once more came alive and understood that it hadn't even been my friend Anton, but his father, who along with Johan had come to my rescue, and then rowed me ashore. All the salt water that had to be removed through both nose and mouth was an unbearable pain. Other than that I recovered quickly from this experience. It wasn't long before I once more landed in no small amount of danger.

It was March. I had climbed up on a some-what fragile part of the fixed winter ice, from which I intended to shoot seals. I built myself a shooting-wall to rest the rifle on out of the loose snow that was to be found. I was soon done with this, and laid myself down to wait, but having waited in vain for a while, grew stiff with the cold, so I got up to flex myself a bit. Just a couple of steps to the left the ice was soft, so I immediately fell in without it being possible for me to get out again. In every place that I reached, the ice broke off immediately. Time and time again I tried to grasp my ice-staff, which stood planted a short distance away in better ice. Each time I lifted myself up to reach out for it, I fell back into the ice hole again (the ice, as mentioned, always broke under my weight). In the end it was with the help of my *Toq* (staff), that I managed to swing myself up. At this point it can definitely be said that I quickly snatched up my tools and scurried home over the ice, which fortunately was firm all the way to our site.

While climbing the hill home, I had to give up. My mother, who had seen me from the window, came down and took me by the hand and led me to the house. This incident took place at Arane, but we later moved to Oqaatsut, where I once again happened to experience something unusual. I hadn't become a seal catcher yet, only fished and shot birds from the kayak. The ponds and puddles had already frozen stiff by October, however an unexpected thaw with stiff winds came up. When we stepped out the door one morning to gauge the weather, the frost had returned and mother immediately wanted to go out to scrape *kiliagkat*.[11]

---

11. *Frozen berries that are scraped up along with the frozen snow.*

As I saw her preparing herself I said: "Mother, there is no point. It would be wasted effort, the berries cannot already have refrozen." She made no objection, but calmly remained at home, while I sped off to shoot eider. I quickly shot four not far from there, and just at the time when I knew that the sun was peeping into our house site, I decided to bring these home, as I also wanted to go out again to obtain a couple of sculpins before evening. There was a lot of chop in the fjord as I laid to. For this reason I pulled the kayak sufficiently far up so that it was safe against the waters, and then quickly ran up with my birds.

The sun was now on the southern wall of our house, and the window was open. I immediately spotted my mother, who comfortably went about in there, humming, all the while busying herself with cooking. When I simply passed the birds in through the window to her, she replied: "But are you not coming in?! What are you up to?"

"No, I have to be off again to pull in some sculpins," I replied, "besides, my kayak is only loosely pulled ashore, so I need to hurry even more." So I ran off, while I heard mother's comfortable tones dwindle in the distance, and furthest from my mind at this moment was the thought that an incalculable danger was so near. The first thing I did when I got there, was to take my oar in hand and pull the kayak in, but it was slippery underfoot. I suddenly lost my balance and fell head first across the kayak. I sought to grab a hold of it, and let go of the oar, but caught it once more. It was now the only thing I had to keep myself afloat. Thankfully my clothes were so water-tight and good that they didn't immediately pull me down. Now it was a question of making myself noticed to those at the site, where only the womenfolk were home at the moment, as all the men were still out hunting. I was, however, only noticed by the site's dogs, each and every one of which came running down. It was unmistakably clear that they would have helped me, if only they could have. They sought to draw people's attention to me by constantly running back and forth between the house and the fjord, and each time the waves pulled me offshore, they leapt towards me. If they felt they were beginning to sink, they would once more crawl ashore and run up outside the houses, where they howled and made a racket, then came leaping down. Once again, even though we humans seem to have come to the border line of existence, rescue can still be found!

I had almost lost all strength, and it was all I could do to keep my mouth above water, as I had grown heavier and heavier from the water eventually seeping into my skins. I also had to put up with swallowing large mouthfuls of salt water, so I now began to prepare myself for what might come and just as I had decied to be patient, it felt exactly as if I passed away, and I no longer felt the battle to draw breath or the cold of the water. On the contrary, I felt a kind of alleviation. It must have been in the same moment that I was freed from death, to be allowed to live until this day—contrary to all merit.

It was the site's children that had luckily spotted my kayak floating about the sea, and immediately summoned my mother, who even thought (she later told me) that I had first capsized and fallen out of the kayak at the same moment she heard news of it. She and the other women had thoughtfully equipped themselves each with a tent-pole, before running down to me. When they spotted me in the middle of the ring of foam that my wallowing body formed in the water, there supposedly was no more of me visible than my hair and fingers, which were clamped cramp like around the oar. From the beach they immediately sought out my armpits with their long poles, and in this way managed to get me a little closer to shore. I still would not have been saved, they said, if mother had not, holding onto the others with one hand, taken a stride out into the surf and, with a foothold on a little rock, grabbed me by the hair. As I was completely unconscious, they had to treat me on the beach, and there I came alive, as soon as they had got me to froth and throw up the sea water.

My waking felt similar to my earlier passing away, it was a dream state—again as if I lay quite alone, half-asphyxiated in the sea, and then felt how I grew warm after first having felt a strong chill. In the end I wanted to shout, but I couldn't utter a sound. When I had regained my strength somewhat, they carried me home in such a way that I walked between two of them with an arm around their necks. It was truly very commendable that these people, who were but poor, weak women, could bring rescue in such a way . . .

As soon as I came inside into the warmth, I grew short of breath but once I grew properly warm beneath the blankets, things improved. Since I still needed an emetic they gave me a tobacco decoction, after which I recovered fully.

We brought our dead back in calm weather.

Accounts from Kagssimiut
Reported by
Peter Motzfeldt

∎

In the spring of 1862 the great ice from the east coast brought a lot of Hooded seals.

On the 14th of April all men went hunting for them. The skies were very cloudy, with squalls from various directions. Cloud cover gradually thickened, and around twelve o'clock, it snowed. Kalarnak and Boas came back then, and I was quite sure that I would also soon see my sons, as they were among the more careful kayakers. As the afternoon progressed though, there was no sign of them, whereas both Marcus and the brothers Herman and Abel came home before evening, Marcus with a large Hooded seal in tow. They wondered why the others had not yet arrived, and they thought they had seen a glimpse of them between the showers at roughly the time when they had finally dealt with their seal; yes, they had given a signal of their catch— they said, and lain still for a short while to wait and see if they were going to obtain their piece of the catch. They waited in vain, eventually setting off homewards, fighting a hard south-westerly. Back home we'd only had a north-easterly, oddly enough, which from time to time veered due north.

Well, should the situation be as bad as having gotten themselves lost, then it was a great comfort they had so many accompanying them: fully seven kayaks from here and even two from Nunarssuit. These nine, who instead of having come home, were now shrouded in the gloom of night, were the following: the two sons of our cooper Thomas and the two of the widow Judith; furthermore Poul, son of Malene, who had been a resident at Godthaab. Poul was without a *kapitak* (storm furs) and had the additional worry of two boils. Finally there were, in addition to the two Nunarssuits, my own poor boys!

Our disquiet increased with every moment, but we finally laid ourselves down, though without sleep coming to our eyes, and at the first light of day I went to the lookout with a pair of binoculars, where Thomas soon arrived. Wind blew steadily and it was quite clear. Gradually most of the residents of the site came up, and we all stayed here, right until we couldn't any longer due to the blowing snow, and there was now nothing else to do than to wait for it to pass.

The storm increased in strength. When it was two o'clock we finally saw a kayak navigate its way in, and people flooded down to the beach to hear news, though I preferred to stay standing outside my house. It was soon shouted up to me that all was well and good, which I immediately passed on, as I shouted up to my married son's house and similarly to Thomas', which lay further up still. The messenger was one of the two from Nuuarssiut. He had left the others far out—he said, and had taken the direct route here, rather than go to his own settlement at Nunarssuit, partially because he wanted to trade with me in the shop, and partially to inform us what he knew about the others.

As we happen to look out of the shop door a little bit later, we see that kayaks again are coming straight in from at sea, this time four in number. It didn't take me long to find out that my sons were not among them, though I quickly comforted myself with the thought that they could not yet be without company, as we were still missing Poul (he was the one without a storm fur) and also one of the Nunarssuits. Those people are all fine kayakmen. Furthermore they could maybe have gone ashore some place or another on the way. I therefore immediately made preparations to have a bite of food as well as more packed down to send with him, because I wanted to send him out to seek among the many inlets around us.

The four approached closer and closer and finally landed. These were Thomas and Judith's two sons, but the news they brought!—the last they had seen both of my sons and the Nunarssuits, far beyond the ice belt, surrendered to a rocking iceberg. Oh, if only we had a steamer—then we might yet have been able to save them!

They told the following story: When the south-westerly had stood straight offshore like a *nunasarnek* (offshore wind), the entire group had started to row homewards in good order. The visibility had, however, already become completely clouded and the land lost from sight. They had the wind from their left and kept it until it fell away completely. It was then they suspected that it had turned, and for a long time they discussed what they were to do now. Whether they should keep the wind, as it was, on their right or left side.

It was here that, oddly enough, all the youngsters had been right (which the later sorrowful results showed), but they had, out of their usual reverence, followed the opinion of their elders, which was the opposite of their own. Meanwhile it grew later and later at night, and they never reached land, for they were rowing, without knowing it, continuously further and further out to sea. In the end they had decided to get up and rest on an ice floe—for they could not see their hands before them in the falling snow.

By the break of day, Judith's sons had wanted to leave again, they said, and they had sought to convince their friends to follow them (at this point the entire group that had left was still together), but none of the others yet had the courage to do so. Only when the seas, which had sent breakers straight across their ice floe all night, had reduced a bit, had they got themselves ready to go to their kayaks again. They had to carry the poor thing with the boil. When his strength finally failed completely due to pains in his arms, to the extent that he could no longer help with his oar, he asked them to release him, as he would rather perish on the spot than remain in his current sufferings. They obeyed and left.

Still, they had no clue whatsoever of how far out they had ventured, since the storm fog hung over land and sea. Only when the sun rose further up in the sky did it clear enough for them to understand that they had strayed far out to sea and were no closer to land than they had Nunarssuit's highest peak, Isugdlek, in such a position that they had to know that they were also despairingly far out to sea. Because of this, the oldest of my sons lost courage to such an extent that he would rather make his way back onto a drifting floe, whereas both the brother, who wouldn't separate from him, and the remaining Nunarssuit, eventually followed.

They said, of this man from Nunarssuit, that he had throughout the trip sought to comfort my sons and exhort them to patience and remember that there was an eye that watched over them. When my oldest son began to complain at the thought of those he would now leave unprovided for, the other answered that this was not the time for such worries, but that one should always have one's own salvation in mind.

Yes, if only we had a steamer on that occasion!

Adventures and Observations on Things I Have Experienced
By
Petrus Lynge–Seal hunter

∎

   The reason I have not provided anything for the "entertainment periodical" before, is that I cannot write properly myself. When I recently sat out, lonely, rowing in my kayak, it struck me that it might be possible anyway, provided my good friend Villads, our catechist, help me correct the errors in my writing, and he certainly could—for he knows nothing of sloth. I myself do not have the sense to be able to place the parts together in the right order, and since my memory isn't the best either, I only remember my experiences periodically. All I recall of my earliest childhood was that we, at home, knew nothing other than good days. Things must have been tight at one point, I think, for I clearly remember how father, along with Mads and uncle Hans one day had to go out to fish for sculpins along with the other catchers from the site. I also remember that they came back with a monstrously large bunch, as they had strung them all on one string . . . that time, when the man we Greenlanders refer to as the big carpenter[12] was made head of a trading post, we Napassoks gained Stefanus as catechist, for Paulus, our original teacher and catechist, was to go with the carpenter and the settling Greenlanders to the new trading post. Both these catechists, Paulus and Stefanus, were of the unlearned kind, as the current teaching facility (the Seminary) did not yet exist in their youth. They therefore could not teach us anything other than how to read, not write or calculate.

It is true that it is enviable to see what children can do compared to back then . . . after the big carpenter had been at Umanak (the newly founded trading post) for two years, it was decided that he was to take over Napassok and my father was, as part of this, to move to the Ikamiut Greenlandic site north of the colony.

We returned to Napassok after only two years. During the last of our winters at Ikamiut, the distress was great, and the Greenlanders practically said that, had Father not been there, things would have gone very badly for them. He took care of them in a fatherly way, partially by each day letting the coffee kettle do a round of all the huts, and partially by allowing people to receive free foods from the stores of the colony shop. He also hosted the men of the site, and forced those that no longer wanted to do

12. *The same Danish carpenter, Williamsen, lost his life during the starvation winter at Napassok (1834-55) by risking his way out to the colony in an umiak to obtain help for the Greenlanders who were in extreme distress. People never learned what had happened to this sad expedition.*

anything other than lay down and die to stop being so indifferent—ordering them to sit upright on the bench during the day. As soon as it was possible, towards the end of the winter, he sent Mads and my uncle Hans to the colony to notify them of the situation here, but they were a long time arriving due to the many detours they had to make because of winter ice blocking the usual kayak route. But when Mads finally came back alone from this postal trip, he brought us even more horrific news: our old Napassok had almost died from starvation during the same winter. He furthermore brought orders from the colony administrator for my father to make his way down there without delay. We then immediately travelled across the colony, which lay mid-way between the two places, one to the north, the other south. We were not allowed to rest for long before we had to hurry on to the distressed place, where temporary aid had been sent under the leadership of my uncle Hans.

I had grown up here and known everyone, yet was to witness the most terrible of sights imaginable. The hungering had, without further ado, made use of the Danish house,[13] as unburied bodies lay all over the place in their own huts, some of which had been thrown down on top of the dead in order to bury them in one go. There had no longer been the strength to bury

---

13. *The property of the trading post manager.*

each body separately. When father asked them to rise, so that he could better see in the light, he found almost all of them unrecognizable. The widow to the large carpenter, who had left in the umiak, but never again returned, was also among these, and her face was, similarly to the others, strongly swollen, and her eyes protruded far out of her head. I have heard from older people that this comes from subsisting purely off the beach (eating seaweed).

The next morning, when my uncle wanted me to join him at our former house, where the survivors had gradually gathered as relatives and other house-mates passed away, I initially wanted nothing of it. I was at the time so excessively touchy about my person that even the smallest cut or hurt made me agitated. I later hardened myself against this: how would I otherwise have become a seal hunter?—this was the year of my confirmation. It was terrible to see them lying spread out over the floor, all skin and bone, and yet Hans said that it was nothing compared to what it had been like when he initially came down.

No sooner had they spotted father than they all began to cry and moan. This would not have happened to them had he only been with them, then they cried and cried some more.

They had peeled off and burnt all the internal woodwork in the stove. A bit of warmth did them some good, they said. When we left the place two years ago, we had left the house in perfect condition, but now there was nothing left of its internal decoration but the panel by my parents sitting and lying spot. We never received any remuneration, though from time to time I heard mention that they considered reimbursing us a bit.

Napassok *("upright")* was previously called Igdlugtalik. The Napassok name originates in an upright stone on the top of a hill. Seen from the south it is similar to a Danish dressed woman, and we picked up the odd habit of saying, each time something unlucky happens or something evil befalls us, such as a death or the like: "It must be her, up there!"

While we were at Ikamiut, I once capsized with my kayak, as I wanted to pull my bird spear out of a piece of ice, where I had stuck it after throwing it at a razorbill that was swimming close beneath. Theofilus, who was with me, helped me up again. When I found the speared razorbill floating on the water on the way back, I didn't fail to take it with me, but at home I was thoroughly told off by my father, in spite of his joy in having me returned unharmed.

Similarly, I also capsized on another occasion when a kayak which our umiak was towing, through their carefree rowing, ran straight into me and knocked me over. To begin with they didn't even notice the damage they had caused, but when I had toppled out of the kayak, they finally became aware of me and took me in the umiak.

Father then forced me to learn capsizing

and righting in the way proper for a true kayak-man. I was close to tears with unwillingness, but I didn't object, for he was my father. He took responsibility for my learning himself and began by tipping me over onto one side as he gripped the bow of my kayak tightly in his hand. When I dallied and could not resolve myself to throw myself round, he took care of it for me and kept me under water for a not inconsiderable amount of time before he allowed me to come out again. In this way he continued the exercises until I got to the point where I practically looked forward to them, and in the end learned how to properly right myself unaided.

I will now give my opinion on exiting and not exiting the kayak after it has capsized. It is my opinion that one, once there is reason to ex-pect help from another kayakman, should avoid crawling out until the latter reaches you, as you make the job much less difficult for the one that comes to help, and causes him much less con-cern for the outcome. Furthermore our own suffering is reduced, as we don't get as soaked and frozen as we do when we have been out of the kayak and in the water. I have had an ex-perience in that regard. It was during the time where I still hadn't quite learned how to right myself unaided.

It was a summer evening at Ikamiut, when, towards sunset I had a particularly great urge to follow Amos, whom I thought had rowed over to Amarkok, but didn't encounter. Since I heard from some fishing kayaks on the way that he had gone all the way to Kornok. I had already come as far as I had, I didn't want to turn around without first having looked into the sound a bit.

It was an irresistible yearning that gripped me, and no sooner had Amarkok opened itself to me than I immediately spotted many seals, nor was I late in harpooning and throwing the bladder. Capsizing was the last thing on my mind at this moment. No sooner had I placed my next weapon in the animal, which had just popped up for the third time, before I immediately capsized. In one single moment I realized that I was alone, and also that it was beyond my power to right myself unless some others came to help, for which reason I sent a farewell thought to my parents as well as to all widows and the fatherless and to anyone who, in the foundered kayakman, loses their life's provider. Then, without knowing how, or whether it was intentional or not, I moved my oar slightly, which I still held under water, and then, in the same moment, to my great surprise, found myself sitting on an even keel, without my kayak even being harmed in the slightest—all equipment, even my kayak gloves, lay in their correct places. I presumably didn't turn upside down at all, as I had believed in my confusion at the time, but simply lain on one side.

Had I immediately crawled out into the sea then I would certainly have been lost, as it is nearly impossible to get oneself into the kayak again in high seas.

Father died in September 1868. Shortly before he died, he once turned towards me on the bench and said: "When I am dead, you must take the boards and nails for my coffin from the Trade's stocks, then not forget to note every little thing you withdraw." I didn't think these words would gain such deep meaning, so shortly after he was dead. He was to me what a mother is to the suckling child. Maybe he also loved me so greatly because I was his only son.

Mother had been married before, and with her came four siblings, of which two are still alive. Yes, it is true that my parents loved me, but for that reason they rebuked and punished me equally when they thought I needed it. That was as it should be, since they were the parents and I, the child. Otherwise I noticed that it has become customary that children do what they want in all things, as some parents excuse them, saying: "Oh, we have to be forbearing with him, since he's a little *akigssak*[14]" and of yet another one: "Oh, it is such a sweet little one." Such a practice is wrong, as one must discipline one's children when needed, otherwise they will have no limitations, and besides, one only has to remember this: "Fathers, discipline your children." Yes, it is true, that only when the parents teach their children according to scripture will they benefit from them.

It grieved me terribly to lose my father, and

14. *The first child born after the death of a sibling.*

not long after that our youngest little girl. This was not the worst of it, and I truly came to understand what I had, on several occasions, heard older people say, which was: it was nothing to lose ones parents compared to losing a spouse. Yes, such true words, for what had my parents passing been like compared to that of my wife! This, and our devotion to one another, I cannot yet bear to speak of. I can only say that it is almost unbearably sad to come home from sea and into this house . . . and then the first wakening in the morning!

When my father died, I immediately sent a letter to the colony, as we were loath to enter winter without a trading post manager. The mail brought back the reply that I could be the one to take care of the shop and the blubber distribution for the time being. How would that go, I wondered. I, who neither knew how to calculate or write properly. I had to try it, and once again trusted in my Villads, and he has truly been my support up until this day. I had been there many times for the weighing and measuring when father took stock of the shop goods, especially when this happened on one of the days where I couldn't go out in my kayak due to the weather, but when I wanted to stand with him in the evening when he was doing his calculations, he always asked me to leave, as it disturbed him to have someone nearby. So I obeyed and left. It didn't matter anyway, for I was surely destined to become a seal hunter. The result of this is that I am still completely ignorant of accounting. Father tended to sum things up every month, but I have also only ever heard him praised (by the head manager at the colony) for his great diligence as a trading post manager.

It is hard to say whom I take after in stupidity. It is bad, truly, when you are stupid, then you never become a quick learner, and I have seen enough to say that clever and dumb are types apart, and have similarly noticed that those who can do something always make themselves beloved. In spite of my lack of learning, I cannot say other than that I have been shown a lot of love. God be thanked for the dear Villads—I can ask his advice at any time and about anything I want, such as now, for example, regarding the designations of the Danish trade goods. Indeed, there is nothing that he does not understand, and on the rare occasion where I can tell him about something that he doesn't know, he promptly understands it due to his great intelligence. It is reasonable that Villads be loved by all on the site, as the one who sated our spirits, but what would that then make him to me, to whom he provided very timely aid?

Consider for esample the accounts alone! When nothing was missing (i.e. there was not a shortfall on the accounts), we really benefited from it, Villads and I, and he would never accept payment for everything he did for me, and since the Danes at the colony were so inclined not to be too strict with me, I had good reason to be pleased with my salary, which by the way I spend sensibly, in part also due to Villads' guidance. I also appreciate all things, and am never averse to letting my countrymen come to trade in the shop, even if it occurs after an entire day's fasting. I go straight up to the shop or the blubber house simply to avoid having them wait for me, and I have also on many occasions had my skin torn from my hands, which aren't among the strongest out there, by grasping the ice cold weights and balances.

I was later also made *Parssissok* (welfare administrator), even though the law said that one needed to have reached one's thirtieth year to become so. "Held in preparedness" (Deputy)— that I'd already been since the year when Jens at Kangamiut was chosen as the assemblyman. At the time I completely and formally took over his place, I was no more than 21 years old, and have now been so for 12 years without replacement, and this year, 1880, I have been re-elected again. Admittedly this time I would rather not have, and I also asked them not to vote for me at the spring meeting at the colony. When Villads immediately mentioned me, everyone else did as well, and when I later asked why they had done it, some replied: "Well, because you are the only one who understands how to do it," and, "who else were we to have chosen?" In spite of my unwillingness, I had to obey the majority, and now I'll presumably never escape before I grow ill or utterly useless, since it seems they will hear nothing of anyone else.

During the main assembly meetings in the spring, I always received the most friendly welcome from my countrymen, for which I truly must praise them highly. Never sour faces when I met them on the roads between the houses, only pure friendliness. Before evening I would generally have received invitations from all—although not entirely everywhere.

When they didn't understand that I was joking, they could sometimes be slightly insulted. For example, when *Angutit* (the kayakmen) stood gathered during our meetings with the Danish leaders, for which we often used a spare room in the church attic, and when they spotted me, they would shout: "Make sure I get something, Petrus—and me too, me too, Petrus"[15]—and then I could reply: "Petrus, do you say? Do you not know that today my name isn't Petrus, but *Parssissok* (the assemblyman—Mr. Assemblyman), they didn't always immediately understand that it was said only in jest (thinking I was pretentious).

When I was at the colony, I always had to stay at Claus' place. This was the custom ever since I was a child, and it was always a great pleasure to stay with them, especially during the good hunting periods. In later years I could have had another perfectly good place to sleep during my visits there, specifically at my uncle Hans' place. Each time I had gone straight in to them, message received immediately after arrival from

15. *The yearly budget surplus, which is distributed to the most meritorious kayakmen according to the recommendation of the native assemblymen of the respective sites.*

Claus's place, saying that I could go ahead and come right over.

I had great fun with my cousins Geert and Salomon. We spoke, laughed and joked and sometimes played cards. On one occasion colony administrator H. and colony administrator L. gifted me a bottle of brandy, which we only used in all decency between us to gamble with, in such a way that the one who won got a shot of Schnapps.

My cousins would not let go of me for a moment, following me everywhere I went. No matter how old I have become, I also prefer to have their company when I wander around from place to place, as I have always been quite bashful.

I crept in again.

On the Sinking of Our Umiak
by
Ignatius

∎

We rowed from home on the 26th of September 1890, and reached the Grædefjord *("The weeping fjord")* in one haul. We left again the next morning and took with us two of Jacob's children, Jonas and Martha.

We reached Sagdliarutsit then Puiatsiait, where we stayed for three days before we went on to Alangordliat. Here the current grew so strong that we had to take the boat ashore and carry it forward to the Nikissa tent site, where we planned to set up camp. Arriving there I let the others set up the tent and set off into the Sangmissok fjord, where I managed to catch two elderly Harbor seals *(natsigdlait)*. The next day Jonas and I went out early to hunt reindeer, and we also managed to fell one, after which we decided to stay the night at that location. When the fjord opened up before us on the return trip the next morning, we discovered that fjord ice had formed on it overnight. It didn't scare me that much, but Jonas immediately said: "Please let us break up camp and leave here—otherwise we'll be frozen in."

I would rather not have, but when, after our arrival at the tent, he repeated the same words, I replied: "Well, then let us see about heading off —maybe you are right in that it could end badly for us otherwise."

The day was noted as the 5th of October, and true enough, new ice had settled here and there, but we felt that this probably wouldn't damage the umiak.

When we were about to climb into it, one of the rowers said: "I would rather not die without first having tasted some of our newly caught reindeer." To this Martha replied, somewhat indignantly: "Who would concern themselves with reindeer meat now—in any case, I am equally unconcerned about dying, as we have our excellent new umiak!"

We rowed and rowed without obstacles until well into the afternoon, when we neared Ikerassak and noticed that a storm was brewing. When we finally approached its mouth, the storm came rushing in with such violence that we all had to let go of what we were doing to point at it, at once exclaiming: "Yes, see, here it comes!"

I immediately turned us into the wind, but we were with equal speed thrown towards an iceberg and simultaneously rammed by the fractured new ice, which the storm carried with it, and the umiak immediately sprang a leak and began to sink. I heard one of our rowers cry: "Won't God, our creator, ever look down on us?" In the rushing of the storm and the loud crashing of the boat I couldn't discern which of them spoke.

Now I, Ignatius, rushed to get my kayak out,[16] but it immediately slipped under one of the many ice floes, from under which I only managed to pull it out with a powerful tug. Jonas and I had barely managed to place ourselves in our respective kayaks before we saw the umiak sink before our eyes.

In the same moment I felt something touch my shoulder from behind, and when I turned I saw that it was Martha. A wave pushed her away again at the same moment, and now we two kayakmen began to sink, ripped by the ice. As we slowly sank into the sea, I heard Jonas pray: "Jesus, come and stay with me, your wounds be my comfort—I love you!" He was the only one of them I heard sing. Of course he was also the one that I, because of my great responsibility, had constantly been aware of.

Now they had all sunk to the bottom—I thought—as I popped up to the surface again, having worked my way out of the kayak under water. It was not so, though I soon after spotted Martha and then Elisabeth, my own wife, and our old servant Priscilla. The others were, and remained gone, along with Jonas—for he, in contrast with myself, had continued to cling to his kayak.

Then Elisabeth says to me: "Well, now God

16. *When a boat owner steers his own boat, he will most usually tow his kayak along in its wake, but will, in exceptional circumstances, such as here in the thin ice, prefer to place it up on the edge of his boat.*

himself will dissolve our marriage through death," and she was then immediately knocked away. Now it was Priscilla and myself who remained alone on the waves. I lifted my hands to the sky and shouted: "God, have mercy on me for my sins!" For I had managed to lift myself with the help of a bundle of skin, which had floated up and which I soon recognized as having been my old mother's. The steering oar also came floating over to me. I kept myself above water to my chest, and later my entire torso. Priscilla appeared once more atop a wave, and I heard her say: "Isn't this terrible? Now it is probably my turn!"

"Yes, you speak the truth when you say it 'is terrible'," I replied, "but which of us, whether it be you or me, is to be punished or pardoned next, nobody knows." Then I repeated my prayer from before. She, the old woman, whom I least would have expected to live, lived the longest. She didn't die until towards midnight, and her death was not by drowning, for she had expired before she sank to the depths. Soon another bundle of traveling clothes came rushing towards me, and I recognized it as being Martha's. I finally managed to get it loosened and took out her little feather blanket, into which I tore a couple of holes so I could pull it over myself. During this work, I hung across a small ice mound. Slightly later a somewhat larger and better floe drifted towards me, and I boarded it and got my items onto it, namely the skin bundles as well as my steering oar. It was no better than that my legs dipped into the water to the middle of the thighs. In this condition the storm pushed me quickly forwards, along with the very fractured ice which now came on fast. I had a hard time keeping myself secure where I sat, and in the end I had to lose my possessions. —I prayed constantly, though I remembered well that God was almighty and would in all circumstances only act according to his own will.

(The rest of his narrative is somewhat lengthy and is abridged.)

Ignatius finally drifted to shore, followed by a number of items from the foundering, including his very battered kayak. In spite of his despairing state, he couldn't thank God enough, he said, and went to the top of a small mountain to make his devotions. After his first sleep, he set about repairing the kayak, for which he made use of the skins that drifted ashore, which had been wrapped around each of the traveling bundles. By cutting these into strips in order to lash the woodwork together, and with a bit of blubber, which could still be found hanging by the cross-straps of the kayak,[17] he was able to plug the tears in the skin cover. His work took him three days, as the repairs still proved insufficient. He worked, prayed, thanked, and won-

---

17. *A kayakman always brings some seal blubber with him on the kayak deck, partially to grab a bite from when hungry, partially to rub his frozen hands with, but especially to plug unexpected holes in the kayak.*

dered, most of all, why he wasn't freezing more than he was, but says that it probably arose from the fact that he was still agitated. When he was finally finished with his preparations, he once more went up onto the mountain and "bestowed all his dead to God." In danger of his life, he then set off across the many broad inlets on the route, among them the broad, clayey Markaksbugt (Markak Bay), which borders the northern coasts of the Grædefjord. The land of the two strangers he had brought away and led to disaster. He could not get Jonas and Martha out of his thoughts, and he could not even persuade himself to set off across the Grædefjord to Jacob's settlement until three days had passed. There, where he was at the time, he encountered a fox trap, which he knew belonged to the same Jacob. He took out the bait, a sculpin, and ate it raw.

Ignatius then finishes the tale himself, as follows:

When I, on the morning of the fourth day, set off across the Grædefjord, I immediately spotted a kayakman the moment I came under the mountains of the Greenlandic site—and who else could it be but Samuel, Jonas and Martha's older brother. It was a terrible moment, but I had to get it over with and rowed right up to him and said: "You must now do with me as you see fit. I deserve—here I am—utterly miserable, the only survivor of all of them—the others are no more—the umiak has foundered."

Samuel was purely dismayed, and his only words were: "You poor thing, you truly are to be greatly pitied."

Such comfort! We now accompanied each other to the site, where both Jacob and his wife received me with no less mildness and kindness than their son had shown. I, who had caused them to lose their two dear children, was not worthy. For this happy outcome too, I had to praise God.

I stayed with these people awhile, until I had more or less recovered from the great accident.

What Happened One Time to the Seal Hunters at Kangamiut

by
Jens Kreutzman

∎

On the 9th of February, after we had previously had a couple of kayak wrecks, Esaias Hosiasin perished on a day of very good weather. People assumed that he must have been crushed between the pieces of the great-ice, without us being sure. When the same great-ice was driven into the fjord, we discovered, among the heaving masses, a human corpse, which in spite of all our efforts we could not get a hold of among the numerous ice blocks, both great and small, which still approached and receded.

Shortly after a number of walruses arrived, which we could not hunt however, so long as the drift ice lay as close as it did. Nor was it long before it dispersed enough for us to get a bit more open water. At that point Simeon and Isak got an animal each, and Isak's was with large unborn young. This was the 22nd of February, and on the 25th the opportunity was even greater, as the current had set the ice well off shore, for which reason six of our best kayakmen immediately went hunting. These were the brothers Isak and Jens, Mads and James, Seth Egede and Adam Joelsen.

They didn't encounter the animals until well into the afternoon. When they finally spotted three of them, they soon caught their scent and retreated northwards. However they later turned back, so Isak once more got one, which, funny enough, just like the previous one he had caught, had live young in it.

Now the easterly wind picked up to such a degree that they could not consider getting the large walrus towed home to the settlement, so they decided to beach it at Kangerdlugssuaq, which was the coast they had closest to hand. When they rowed in they could already see, from some distance, that the sea was breaking too heavily, so they set off towards Tassingortarssuak instead, which they reached on a receding tide. At this point it had grown quite dark, but they still managed to haul the walrus up onto the beach and began to flense it, but only in such a way that, each time the sea came rolling in, they had to withdraw from their work and run up to the hills. When they eventually managed to get the skin off, and the carcass divided into pieces, the task became to get all of this carried sufficiently far from the sea where it was safe from its penetration, as they now quickly had to head off. However it was already too late for that—it was no longer possible to get into the kayaks, for the south-westerly had arrived and was already starting to bring rain. Now they stood without even the slightest bit of shelter as this island was, unfortunately one of the smooth, round ones without cliff-faces that the snow might drift against, and they could not obtain even the slightest wall of drifted snow, so had to settle for seating themselves on the ground back to back, to retain a bit of heat.

The sea came rolling into shore stronger and stronger, and was once on the verge of carrying James' kayak away with it, but his older brother managed to grab a hold at the last moment. They now had to withdraw further due to the sea spray, and in doing so had less shelter than they had had before, but there was nothing else they could do other than wait for the morning of the next day. They tried, to the best of their ability, to dig down into the thin layer of snow which covered the island, as well as to scrape together a bit of loose snow with which to raise the mound around them. It was impossible though, as the storm whipped away again with equal speed.

The first part of the night passed tolerably. Then came the dawn and froze them with strong gusts from the west, and the seas were just as heavy. Nonetheless they had now resolved themselves to do their utmost to get off the island, as they would otherwise freeze to death in their soaking and frozen clothes. Now they walked along the fjord to see if there might be a place where they could get out to sea. The only place was at Angnikitsunguak.[18] They then

18. *Angnikitsunguak always means a stone or rock formation which is broad at the top, but runs to a point below. Is often used as a place name.*

headed there, bringing their kayaks with them. En route Seth accidentally struck his kayak against a rock, by which the point broke and twisted itself lopsidedly. They all said it would have been the world's most laughable sight, had the moment not been so serious and they not each preoccupied with the miserable conditions. They were already so exhausted at this point that Jens (who must have set off alone) was found lying with his face in the dirt at the edge of a water-course, in which he would have drowned, had he not lain so still as if he were already dead.

It was Adam that found him.

When they finally reached the place at Angnikitsunguak, Mads offered to be the first man to be pushed off into the sea, then he got into his kayak, tied himself around his neck, hands and waist so the water couldn't penetrate the kayak anywhere, and succeeded in getting out to sea unharmed. Isak fared similarly, although somewhat less adroitly, as he fell on his side with his kayak. Since he was agile, he quickly righted himself once more. Now it was James' turn, and Adam was to push him out, but just as James had made himself ready for it, two heavy waves struck them, and Adam would certainly have lost his grip on James' kayak, had he not had the luck to, with his other hand, grab a crack in the rock by which they were situated. Before they had even managed to recover from this dousing, a third wave came, worse than the two previous ones, and properly tore the kayak away. Adam immediately picked up speed towards the breakers, but they all dashed after it and, in the last moment, managed to get a hold of it. In doing so they suffered another deluge, in which Adam was on the verge of being washed away. James had now had more than enough, and rushed out of his kayak as fast as he could, and they all agreed that the attempt was too dangerous to repeat. They went back again to seek a bit of shelter. But Mads and Isak, who could now not reach shore again, rowed away and told those at home that it had been a terrible moment for them, when they had to leave their friends in distress, and that they had shed tears over this. The sea had also robbed them of their walrus, both the meat and the skin!

Now they proceeded to discuss their miserable condition. Clothes hung around their waists, frozen solid. They once again set to work building a bit of a snow wall around them, after first plugging the holes in their clothes with peat mulch and frozen heather, which they scraped out of the snow. Then they settled down, with the exception of Seth, who knew that it would surely spell the end of him, were he to do so. He therefore preferred to wander about a little yet, and reached the opposite end of the island, from where he decided, after a period of consideration, that they ought to risk another attempt at getting away, no matter how ugly the place looked. It consisted of a cleft or rill, which led straight down from the center of the island to a steep drop, which would absolutely not have been usable at low tide, since the slope would have been too high to plunge across, but which might be passable at high tide. He therefore turned around immediately to notify his friends. After taking one look at them, he didn't really expect much, he said. He demanded that they (to avoid wasting time) immediately take their kayaks. They were so tired and indifferent that— even when they, after much thought, decided to follow him—would not obey him, but saved themselves the trouble until they had seen what they thought of the new site. Then he managed to convince them, so they had to turn around to get their kayaks anyway, which they in no way had the strength to carry, as they were supposed to, on their head, but simply dragged them along the ground, as they wobbled like drunken men against each other.

When they saw the place it made them shudder. At the same time they could not help but admire the wonderful cleft, which was as if intentionally shaped for a kayak's keel. It was Seth's thought that they should seat themselves in their kayaks up on the hill and then slide all the way down along the cleft and then let themselves plunge down over the drop. It was a dangerous ordeal in any case. They did consult each other for a long while before making their final decision, and they spoke as follows: "We know that we can't survive another night here on the island in our poor, frozen clothes—and furthermore we know that if today is not slated to be the day of our death, then no breakers will steal our strength. Let us at least try!" Seth began, but suffered terribly of dizziness during the slide—he said. He fell into the sea without taking any damage other than getting a bit wet, as he hadn't tied his waist completely secure. Adam and James were similarly lucky, and now only Jens remained—the only one of them that would not have got up unaided, had he capsized during the descent. They waited very tensely for him, but he was also lucky and entered the sea properly. Now they spoke joyfully of their great luck in time of need and how they could already feel the warmth return to their lower bodies since Jens had gone under water (in the kayak). They rowed away, wreathed in snow flurries and freezing fog, and arrived here some time after seven o'clock.

The first two had already arrived home at three o'clock. The rest of us didn't get to bed all night, simply so we could sit up and hear them tell of their wonderful salvation. Seth had to be bled the next day and could not go out kayaking for a long time. In almost the same moment that they landed, the great-ice set in in all corners and stayed for a long time before it retreated again, and had the wind not been as variable as it had been for the last day, but instead remained due south-west, Kangamiut would have suffered six serious kayak losses at once, in addition to that of Esaias Hosiassen's earlier in the winter.

The Narration of a Holsteinborger on One of His Hunting Trips

By
Jens Baggesen

∎

Then I saw the moon slip down behind the island
and thought: I wish I were on that island there!
Then I could truly know:
From what, how large and round, how yellow it is!

Since I am here to speak about my life, I will
begin with an example of my childish incom-
prehension and imagination.

I had a strong taste for all there was in the
sky, and desired above all else to have the stars as
toys, as I thought that this was their main purpose, and that had I simply been able to lash our
tent-poles together, so they were long enough
to stand on for the duration, then it would be a
simple matter to make them fall to earth. How
dearly I wanted to touch both the sky and the
distant blue mountains! Many other children
may think the same, and this presumably comes
from the fact that we so often hear talk of the
sky, but in a way incomprehensible to us.

Immediately after I had started to go to
school, I had a strange dream. One day a man
comes, takes me by the hand and leads me away
with him. I would have liked to have known
what he wanted with me, but I was too shy to

ask. When we arrived in the middle of a large plain, where I spotted a pretty, fine house, I said: "Whose is this?" And he replied: "Because your mind yearns for Jesus, you must visit there."

How I rejoiced that I was to see my Savior! The house was not like other houses, but round and so pretty that I almost didn't dare look at it. Now the one that held my hand opened the door and asked me to go in, but he stayed standing outside. Inside the Savior sat and smiled at me, without a word. He was so wonderful, both his face and his garb, that I felt no fear when I saw him, but rather hopefulness. Then I happened to look down at myself and suddenly discovered how dirty and ragged my clothes were, I couldn't help but be terribly ashamed. This persisted the longer I stood there, and I could not achieve peace, but twisted and turned to all sides, until in the end I practically retreated into myself in shame. Just as I was most unhappy with my raggedness, He finally began to speak for the first time and said: "You mustn't be so unhappy about your poor clothes: I have sent word for you so that you might get to know yourself—so that you may live; for I hold the heart of man in my hand, as you have also recently felt, since you were ashamed about your wretched clothes before me—I tell you this—you should not worry."

I was joyful, and now finally dared to divert my eyes from the spot I stood. The insides of the house had no corners and was made of clear mirror glass. Part way up, a shelf ran all the way around, and it was filled with texts that lay arranged in bundles. I asked for a book to read, but he kindly replied: "Nobody was to read of these, and that they were for himself alone." Then I replied: "The heart of man is in your hands." He let me see what the text looked like. Some was written in red letters and some in black, and most were black. I would have liked to have stayed there for much longer, but my companion once more opened the door and led me out. Just as he took my by the hand again I unfortunately woke up.

I wish others would take this, my dream, to heart. It is easy enough to understand, now that one is no longer a child. A more upright Christian than I might put it to much use and warning. As far as I am concerned, it is true that I have often forgotten its warning, and sin is my steady companion, but I will not forget the dream itself for as long as I live.

Aspiration is useful

It may well have been that it was enjoyable to go reindeer hunting during the good times, when there were plenty of animals. Could it still be said so now!

Later—after the good time was over—an immense urge came over me to leave. All others had already travelled to the fjords, and I did not own an umiak. There was nothing else for me to do than to travel on foot, and on the 10th of June Maria and I set off alone from Kerrortussût *("the big stone walls")*. There was still a lot of snow on the ground in places, so we had to go up and walk along the mountain ridges instead of taking the usual route round the bottom. Although we did have to go down once, and that was when we reached the bottom of the fjord, after we had gone far enough east. The large snow spots in the hollows of the mountainside were as soft and tender as foam. We held each others' hands and let the sliding begin until we reached the bottom. We had become drenched in the soft snow and now the fog came in too, and the sky started to look dirtier and dirtier.

By the time we had reached the bottom of Kangerdluarsuk it definitely looked like bad weather. The great river was at its greatest strength and was not even traversable at its outer mouth into the fjord. For this reason we lit a fire where we were and cooked ourselves a meal while we awaited the tide to drop in order to use the beach as a crossing point. When the time was right, we did indeed happily make it across to the other side, where we set ourselves up for the night.

The next day brought nice weather, so I immediately felt the urge to take a look for reindeer at Isunguak, without spotting so much as a single one. So we set off the same evening and continued our walk far into the night, right until we reached the bottom of the Tasserssuak inland lake, until we had also put the river, which dropped into this lake from further up, behind us. Only then did we lay ourselves to rest. There was no sleep though, due to the great mosquito swarms that plagued us.

We were actually supposed to have crossed one more mountain before settling down, since I knew from previous expeditions that was a good sleeping spot. When we reached there, the mountain had been wreathed in fog and it began to drizzle. We preferred to break up camp again and wander across the mountain, and we reached the spot I wanted to find. It was wonderfully dry in the cave, so we slept well. We had hoped to wake up to dry weather, but it poured all day and the next one as well. Only on the third day could we proceed along the Isortuarssuk Lake, where I knew the wild geese tended to reside. We acquired an excellent sleeping spot below an overhanging slope with a lot of grass under it, so we didn't need to erect any walls around us—it was cozy sitting sheltered and watching the raindrops fall in the inland lake.

Still, we couldn't leave the space due to the incessant bad weather for two whole weeks, and we didn't have any other food than the geese I could catch. As soon as the weather improved a bit the geese flew away, and since we were now approaching our third week, I was worried that my wife would literally begin to starve, and she so dearly wanted to go down to Sarfanguak, in the hope that she might see people there. I obeyed her but when we reached the great river, it was so full that it had completely burst its banks, so there was no question of wading in it. Since we were just as incapable of crossing the steep slopes of Ivnajuagtok, we were once more forced to turn northwards. It was not without reason that I feared starvation, but to comfort her I said: "A father does the best he can to prevent his children from suffering want. Would God then forsake his own creations? No, he would not let us die of hunger here."

Above Igangnak, which we ascended from the south side, I saw two ptarmigans, which I shot, then cooked and ate them. All that day I hunted for reindeer, but once again only caught two ptarmigans, which we cooked at sunset. The next day I finally got a reindeer at the top of Pisigssarfik. We had now made it to the 28th of July without having seen any animals before then. It was about time: no sooner had I picked us a spot east of Pisigssarfik, before bad weather set in again, with some snow and night frost. A thin ice laid itself across the small lakes and rivulets. We would actually have frozen badly, had we not had the reindeer. When I got as many as three the next day, what happened to starvation then?

The worst thing now was my fear of leaving Maria home alone while away. I constantly imagined that some wild animal would come and tear her to death, so I was never truly happy before, on approach, I could see that everything was fine at home. Sometimes she also came out with me.

We gradually managed to dry a lot of the meat and lived quite well. One beautiful day, after it had rained for several days in a row, we sat at home together. I lay in front of the pot and blew on the wet heather which didn't want to burn, and Maria sat next to me patching footwear. Suddenly she says: "There's a *kulavak* (reindeer cow)!" I immediately began to rub my eyes, which were running heavily because of the heather smoke. When she began to laugh, I thought that she simply had the better of me, and didn't look around at all. After a bit I couldn't help myself, and saw the large animal flee along with a smaller calf. I noted that they were headed in a southerly direction, and immediately the next morning headed out to find them, and did finally get both of them—with the same shot. I had now, by the way, grown tired of this area, for which reason we placed our dried meat into the *kimatulivik* (mountain hiding place for temporary storage of collected supplies) that we had set up.

We had at this point, mileage-wise (not including my hunting jaunts), wandered about 15-16 miles. We could probably have walked less, had it not been necessary to make the long detours around the inland lakes, or to go all the way over the mountain ridges when we left during the snow's thawing period. We had still had a wonderful time all through the summer, and overall were out as long as the other reindeer hunters. I had now caught ten animals, whose meat we would see about getting down to the fjord. I also wanted to go across to the other side of the river to look down into the bottom of Isortok *("muddy, unclear")*, where the reindeer hunters tend to have their bonfires. When we seriously thought about traveling home with all our animal meat, we had to go back and forth many times, each of us with large pelts around our necks. Yes, we worked hard from morning to evening, but things had been so good for us, so good, apart from the very start, when there was a danger that we were going to starve to death far from other people, especially when the forcefulness of the river prevented us from wading across to Sarfanguak. I do not deny that I was miserable on behalf of my Maria.

Now on the way back—how different the same river was! All the stones in its bed were now partially visible (after all the snow had melted and run out into the fjord), and we had plenty of food, so all concerns for the future were gone. We calmly settled down for awhile, as I wanted to get a reindeer bull in order to bring some more tallow home. I was certainly lucky and got a really fat one, but since I shot it in a place that we were going to have to pass anyway on our return trip, I simply covered this catch thoroughly and went home to Maria empty-handed. The next day we began to head straight home (nardlumuinak). Since we had our great load with us, we went past the previous day's catch, as we didn't want to make a stop before we had reached the northern bank of the Isortuarssuk lake, where we would sleep the coming night. The next day I went back alone to retrieve the bull. The night after that we endured mosquito swarms, the like of which we had never seen.

It was almost impossible to breathe because of them. No matter how well we had plugged all openings to our sleeping place in the mountain gorge, they still managed to find a way in, if not by other routes, then by creeping down through random small holes in the skins we had spread over us as a roof. I tried to smoke them out, but they filled nose and mouth anyway, and we got no sleep at all. The night was so wonderfully calm for them!

As morning approached, I thought of lighting fire to the heather peat—as close to our heads as was feasible—so that the steady smoke might keep them away from us. Then we lay and heard how they fell, dull and heavy, onto the skin over our heads. Later, when we came outside, we saw how the tallow, which we had put down and spread across the cliffs, was completely sprinkled with dead mosquitoes. They looked like small piles of ground coffee beans. Indeed, I have travelled a lot around the inner fjords, but still I have never seen anything like it.

How wonderful it was, when we began to approach the mountains of our home no longer seeming completely blue in the distance. I had decided that our next long term resting spot was to be the outer tent site of Kangerdluarssuk, in part to dry some more of our meat, since the fresh, damp meat was far too heavy to carry,[19]

19. The load of meat is swaddled in the reindeer skin, which is lashed with carrying straps; these are then either placed around the forehead or over the shoulders.

and in part because I wanted to go hunting again—I would surely manage to come out to retrieve it later in the autumn, so that now I only had to hide it away.

I hunted for several days, but saw nothing at all, with the exception of some older tracks of a single galloping animal. This was at the top of Isunguak. After staying for two days we decided to move on. I, too, gradually began to long to see other human beings again, and besides, we were already in the middle of August! It would be necessary for us to make a few return journeys to our resting site. There were probably as many as two good hides for each of us, in addition to what we had taken with us right away.

We started at sunrise, and by midday we had made it to the large cave which those who travel these parts during the summer like to choose as a sleeping place. We set ourselves down to rest, myself with my food on top of a rock, highly satisfied. Just as I am getting comfortable, I hear a strange heavy sound, exactly as if a stream ran deep beneath the stone. We ignored it and carried on until we were done—but imagine this! East of Ujarasugssuak, a family of bears lies, and it must have been one of those whose growling I'd taken to be that of a river.

As I was saying: when we finished eating, we strolled further and rested when we needed to do so. Now, it so happened, since we were to be only porters that day, I had left the gun and hunting bag behind. When Maria, whom I always had walk in front of me, since she wasn't entirely well, had crossed a water course, she spotted something big and white up against the cliff side. As we quietly stand and look at it, several bears begin to move. I had nothing at all to scare or beat them with, were they coming towards us! Maria turned to me and said: "Why on earth did you leave your gun behind?" and since I couldn't provide an answer, said: "Oh, if they wished to harm us, then they would probably have risen by now." When we passed the place on the return journey they were no more than a gun shot away, and had they, lying there on their bellies, only lifted their heads, they would have seen us immediately, but they lay exactly as dogs might: close against one another. We only saw two clearly, by the way, with the third almost hidden by those at the front. We did not want to flee and went over and retrieved our last load. When we had to go past there again, going as far around them as possible, they still lay there. We could not help but keep turning around to look at them. The closer I got to my gun, the more my confidence grew.

It was now as if I no longer was alone, but as if I had been joined by a number of other men. I still let my wife walk ahead of me, since she had got a sore chest from the overexertion of hauling. In spite of us not yet having lost sight of the bear mountain, though we had indeed reached quite a distance away from it, I decided to set up camp for the night, as not only had night fallen, but a thick fog as well. We were not entirely at ease, however, and we could not fall asleep due to the thought of the bears, even though I had placed my gun and two sharp knives at the ready, so that I could quickly grab them if anything came. In the end Maria fell asleep properly. Just as I had fallen into a pleasant doze well into the morning, she woke in alarm, and I immediately rushed outside and looked around. We were certain that something was rustling close by. The fog still hung thickly, but we packed up anyway and just finished getting ready to set off as the fog began to lift. Our burdens were terribly heavy, even though we still hadn't brought everything with us. Well on our way we heard the bears rumbling north of us, but it was not that dangerous, since this was the foggy side and we were hidden from them. Eventually we judged by the sounds that they headed off in a westerly direction, from which we understood that they, luckily, had chosen the northern side of the Kangerdluarssuk fjord, while we were to wander along its southern shores. That night we rested at Ekavdlivik.

It was no laughing matter when we first spotted them, as I didn't have the slightest thing to protect my little wife with. Had I wanted to run away, even just far enough to find a stick (from the thickets that grow plentifully within the fjord valleys), they would immediately have been able to leap on her. It is probably foolish to fear the animals, who might themselves be afraid of us. The animals do not only fear man, but should be subservient to him. Nevertheless, it cannot be denied that one is reluctant to tackle bears, especially during the summer, where they are known to be very nasty.

Had I only been alone! Strange to think that, when we wandered between the fells, far into the lonesome distance, where no human voice was heard, nor even so much as the gun-shot of a reindeer hunter—we were never threatened by danger, which I had feared, and which only now caught up with us in the vicinity of human residences. Each evening, before we laid ourselves down to sleep, I read in our prayer book, and each morning I would go hunting and walk about carefree all day. When I spotted our little homestead from a distance, it is true that I could grow anxious as to how she was faring, but when I came close enough to see her wandering about dabbling around the smoking fire, I couldn't thank my creator and provider enough.

When we left our last night quarters at Ekavdlivik (the salmon river of the Kangerdluarssuk fjord), we decided that we wanted to get home inside of one day's travel, and we therefore unburdened ourselves of a share of the load before we climbed the Manilak fell. After we had covered the meat and skin with big rocks, which we wanted to leave, we walked on unceasingly, and reached Karrortussut around the time when the sun had begun to hide itself away. As soon as our own fjord had opened before us, I fired the gun to see if people were home down at the site. There was no reply, and even when the actual site with the winter houses came into sight soon after, we immediately understood that people were still away on their summer journeys. This was disappointing for us, who had so yearned, and had furthermore not known the smell of coffee for most of the summer. The next morning was my first time to the lookout spot, and what was the first thing I saw, other than the sail of a boat rising over Kitdlinguit? Now it was time to use my voice, for which reason, with all my might, I began to shout: "Boat, Boat!" Poor Maria, alarmed, rushed to the window. Since she had not heard what I had shouted, she thought I had lost my mind. The boat was Thaarup's on its return journey (from its visit to the colony at Holsteinsborg). Now we had ample opportunity to barter our tasty goods—which are equally cherished by Greenlanders and Europeans—for goods from the trade's shop!

From this one sees that, even if you don't own an umiak, you can obtain warm clothes for the winter, if you are prepared to be diligent.

Food and drink and clothing do not come to us of their own accord. We must not lie idle. Now there may well be those that answer: to do as you do is pointlessly arduous; we will wait until there is another hunt! But remember that the number of seals are declining, and that, over all, not as much is caught anymore. No, we must each take advantage of the moment when supplies can be gathered. He who will not do that, must expect to starve.

On the Danger that Amase's Son Joel was Put in Around the Time He Started to Hunt with a Bladder
By
Ungaralak

∎

One year, when the strong southerly wind had already set in the great ice soon after Christmas, both Joel's father and uncle earnestly urged him to shed his usual recklessness while the ice still lay so close, since he knew how his mother worried about him. The rest of us older kayakmen caused the quite young hunters a number of troubles and worries on occasions like this, but with Joel it was an entirely different matter: he really was quite an unusually skillful youngster.

This time we had the drift ice right up against the shore. One morning, somewhat more dispersed and further from land than usual, we all gained a strong urge to get in our kayaks to look around. Besides, we all needed somefood. My house now owned some stashed winter stores, but ones that we had not been able to reach because of the blocking ice.

The weather wasn't the best, being bitingly cold and windy, some times with flurries of snow. The freezing fog hung low and wet over the sea.

However, we had to go, no matter what, though we elders in no way forgot that we had to be constantly vigilant, and said to each other: "Yes, there is no point in charging in blindly, let us simply carefully try our luck, even if it might be in vain, and we obtain nothing."

Hinriggi, Konrad and I were the first ones out. When it didn't look like we'd catch anything, we began to consider turning back again. Then, just as we were most dispirited, we suddenly heard cheerful voices behind us exclaim: "No, let us please row out a bit further—the prospects will probably be better there." We were cheered by these words and quickly hurried after the ones who had spoken. These were Moritz and Joel from our own site and three additional strangers from Sagdlit *("foremost")*. I was still not so careless that I forgot to think of wind and weather, and also reminded my friends of the time of year.

At Nalerka, Joel left us, turning homewards again, which wasn't that strange and for which reason I didn't think any further about it, but continued rowing after the others, who had vanished from my sight behind some high ice. When I shouted to ask how things were behind the high icebergs and floes, they immediately replied that things didn't look too bad with regard to the drifting of the ice, and that there were a good number of troughs, but that there were just as few seals visible there as where we had first laid in wait for them. To which I replied again: "Yes, when the great ice is in, we know we can't expect anything else in the Nalerka area." When we then all got out of our kayaks and climbed up on one of the larger floes, we obtained quite a good view out across the entire ice and gained confirmation that there were quite a few open troughs in our immediate vicinity, whereas the great-ice lay closely clustered out at sea.

We couldn't help but frolic a bit in the troughs and didn't give up hope of a catch, to explain why our stay wasn't all that short, but when we saw that the sun was starting to sink, we said, downheartedly: "No, there isn't anything worth waiting for here any more," and we turned homewards.

When we eventually reached an unusually thick cluster of ice, after rowing for quite awhile, Moritz made us aware that shots could be heard from the center, and we quickly understood that a kayakman must be trapped there—perhaps even Joel. I didn't really think it could be him, based on the direction I had seen him take when he rowed away in the morning. In the same moment we became stuck upon it and had to climb up onto one of the floes until the currents once more split the ice, and we had to wait a good while before we again dared to risk ourselves and our kayaks.

As one of the oldest of the site, I knew the currents here well, and if it was as I presumed, I probably dared pilot us home. Once again, a couple of shots were heard from inside the ice cluster, across from Itussortok. Even that, like all other land, was obscured by the tall ice. It was now certain that one of our young kayakmen was caught and very anxious about the coming night. In spite of the great sympathy we felt for him, we rowed on, since we could do nothing for him, and we would only risk ending in the same state.

Shortly afterwards Moritz took his bearings from some known points in the mountains above our settlement which had now briefly come into sight, since he wanted to make an attempt at breaking straight through the ice cluster. I talked him out of it though and convinced him to follow the rest of us the other way, which I thought to be best. This involved us first going a bit back around until we could reach the trough that I assumed the current, by packing the ice so closely together, must have left along the coast. In the end it grew completely dark, and it was sad to think of the trapped kayaker. We rowed and rowed, and when we, along the predicted trough, reached the height of the cluster from which the shots had sounded, although we now had it on our opposite side, we heard, to our fright, a voice shout quite clearly from inside: "Is that you?"

"You reply, Moritz, your voice is most powerful," I said, and Moritz shouted: "Yes, yes, it is us!" Then added, "I must try to get him." He rushed away from the rest of us and in a moment vanished behind the nearest ice. "Yes, if you reach him, then just stick to my outer route!" I then shouted, and David and I rowed onwards. We both wanted to get home, myself in particular, as the children always grew distressed whenever I stayed out for even a bit longer than usual.

We had seriously dreaded being questioned by Joel's family, but thankfully avoided this, as, of course, we were not the last ones expected in. Moritz was still out, and it was he that Joel had accompanied when he left home in the morning.

I was restless and had to go outside every few moments to see whether someone might appear from the sea. When I finally spotted something, it was only a lonely kayak, which appeared from behind one of the large floes. You should have heard Apolonia's voice, as she shouted out to the kayak: "Has Moritz seen anything of my son Joel?"

How her body trembled! She trembled so much she had to sit right down on the ground, and there she sat as I walked into my house. After I had laid myself down, I was kept awake by pangs of conscience. Then I came to think as follows: "A human's life is like smoke; he knows that death awaits him. He does not govern himself, but has an almighty leader and provider above him." After this I was at peace and fell asleep, but awoke early in the morning when I heard shots. This was Joel's father, who, in spite of being almost blind after an arduous trip he had endured last autumn, had sneaked up to our highest lookout mountain, from which he, using his gun, wished to let himself be known to his son out on the ice. He no longer received a reply, and it was pitiful to see how dejected he was after the fruitless, strenuous journey up to the lookout, to which he must have had to practically crawl on all fours to reach.

At the time when I came outside, Josva too was on his feet, intent on going up to the lookout to fire shots, steadfastly determined to delve into the ice if there were even the slightest signs of life out there.

The skies were overcast. After some time had passed, two kayakmen from Sagdlit came ashore at our site, and they said that they had, from the south side of the ice masses, heard a voice shout out: "Are you ever going to come and rescue me?"

Now we didn't hesitate for a moment; I brought my water-skin over-trousers, since one never knew whether they might be needed. Then I initially wanted to take his father's kayak, but in the end chose Kristoffer's, which was the lightest at the site. For the journey would not purely be across water, so it was a good to have a light kayak when one needed to carry it across the ice floes.

Our haste was now so great one might have thought us refugees. When we reached the bottom of the lookout hill, where Josva stood, letting off signal shots, he answered our enquiry by saying that he had received no reply at all. According to what the men from Sagdlit had reported, there was probably no more than half a mile to the enclosed place from which they had heard the voice. Unfortunately we soon encountered dense and heavy pack ice, so there was little else we could do but stop where we were. Josva then got up on a floe to look around, and when he had stood there scouting for a moment, he suddenly said: "I can see a black point moving." "It can only be him," the rest of us said, and I added that he should make an estimate of the land, so that we could know our direction, should we get lost in the ice. "Imagine" —I added—"if we could give the poor, anxious parents a little hint that he was still alive! We are no further away than they might be able to hear and understand us—there is a loaded gun in Kristoffer's kayak—I'll let off a shot and the rest of you all shout at once with all your might: 'Joel is alive!'"

When we had seen how people began to move ashore, we hurried on as best we could, straight in to the very worst of it, as we let Josva, who was both the most agile and eager of all of us, take the lead. We pressed on in haste, and we did not care that the kayak skins might tear or that the oars might break.

Soon Josva needed to get up on the ice to scout further. "Yes, now I clearly see that the black thing is a person," he said. When I answered that it was strange that this person didn't move to approach us, Josva began, as a result, to worry about the condition in which he might find his nephew. When we later got close enough to him that we assumed that he must be able to hear us, we agreed to shout to him to ask how things were. This again was Josva: *"Kanok inerpit?"* (I wonder how you are). Instead of answering, they simply started to make some strange gestures, so Josva grew even more afraid than he was before, thinking that Joel might have lost his mind. Then I reminded him that Joel had sat out, first all day yesterday, then all night until now, without food or drink, and without having used his voice, so his throat might be so rusty and dry that we possibly couldn't hear what he said. When we finally rowed back and forth and began to approach him by a circuitous route, Josva shouted again: "Well, how are things with you? You're probably freezing horribly."

I didn't hear any reply now either. The others shouted back to me: "He says that he hasn't quite given up on himself." Then we again shouted that he should in no way waste his strength on unnecessary exertions in trying to reach us, since we would soon be there. We then let Hinriggi stay behind on a floe as a marker for the way back, while the rest of us made our way to Joel. When we reached an ice barrier, I chose to dismount onto a floe.

Those who finally reached him had soon realized that it would be no easy task to get him moving and brought home. While I was alone, I had sought out the best place for climbing on my floe and stood ready to point it out to the others. As soon as Josva spotted me, he shouted: "Grab a hold quickly when he comes by, as he's on the verge of sinking." I replied that I didn't think that the kayak lay quite that low; however it quickly turned out that Josva was right. Joel was on the verge of sinking, and it was all we could do to run him up onto a little ice mound, which luckily lay right against the big piece on which I stood. As I now had to make do with pulling him up by his hands, I became highly aware of his unhelpful and exhausted state. There was little strength. Following a hasty examination of his clothes, we discovered that his fabric trousers were wet and icy and that his boots were full of water. Though he was otherwise not particularly sensitive to the cold, he was shivering all over. He recounted that, yesterday, when he felt that he was beginning to get stuck in the ice, he rowed ahead blindly, without calmly considering things, as he should have. He had exposed himself to the worst, so it hadn't been long before his kayak had begun to take on water. When darkness simultaneously began to fall, there had been nothing else for him to do but climb up on a piece of ice and sit there in the kayak. He had frozen terribly, especially his feet, which would probably have frozen off, had he not taken off his upper fur and wrapped it round them. This had been of great benefit, he said.

Now that we all had finally gathered, I said to Josva: "I see that you are wearing two shirts, so take the outer, blue one off, and we will wrap it around his legs beneath the water-skin (old seal skin) over-trousers that I've brought with me." All the men wore caps lined with fur—those we intended to wrap around his feet. This change of clothes, in the middle of the great ice, was indeed a somewhat dangerous affair, but we protected him as well as we could by placing ourselves as close around him as possible. When we were done, we had to get started on his rather damaged kayak, on which no less than three whole lanyards were spent on lashing tears and breaks in the woodwork. We didn't finish setting off before the sun was well on its way towards setting. Josva was to row in front to find a way, and Hinriggi brought up the rear, while I was to row right next to Joel, both to keep an eye on the lashings and to break apart the small ice that might get in Joel's way.

In the end I was sore in both my back and limbs from the twisted position I constantly ended up in. We were all completely stuck in it, and had to get out and up onto the ice, where I, sweaty from the difficult work of ice breaking, now began to freeze quite horribly, which didn't improve during our later slow travel in the pitch blackness. At this point we couldn't resist speaking harshly to Joel, and said: "This is all your fault. Why do you never follow the advice of experienced people?"

He showed himself so repentant and unhappy that he didn't dare look up, to which we immediately felt sympathy for him, stopped and helped him the best we could. It was midnight by the time we made it home.

On the Kivitok Question
by
Hans Rasmussen

∎

During the first period that I was a catechist at Narssak, there were quite a few kayak
accidents. After that, several years passed without
any. Then came the spring of 1883. The 3rd of
March began with good weather and southerly
winds. We were to celebrate the day of suffering
of our lord Jesus Christ, but nevertheless most of
the kayaks had gone out early in the morning.
At the time we were to go to the service, it began to get windier, and just as we had properly
begun, the door suddenly opened, and I heard
something said through it, but without understanding what it was. At roughly the same time,
I saw one of the womenfolk faint, and I gestured
for them to remove her while continuing the
sermon. When we came outside after the service, we learned that Setherak (little Seth) had
foundered quite close outside (it was his wife
that, upon being told the news, had fainted during the service). His comrades had managed to
lay him ashore, however.

While they had been sitting behind the
headland awaiting the eider migration, they had
discovered that Setherak was in the process of
going northwards, when a wave, at that same

moment, broke over him, without him reemerging. One of them had immediately hurried over to the spot, but found him drowned, and they all rowed over to bring the corpse ashore. The weather was, at that point, already too rough for them to be able to bring him back to the site. Our first attempt at bringing him home overland did not succeed either. We only managed to bring him in later in the afternoon. I myself had not been able to go due to a bad abscess. Such sorrow for the mother! Her younger son had not even acquired a kayak yet. But the holy day had been abused, regardless of the fact that God has given us the serious task of honoring each of them, the important ones in particular.

On the 1st of November I was up unusually early and was present when most of the kayakmen set off, Enok among them. As the day progressed, the weak easterly wind died off and I suddenly felt the urge to do a little hunting in the valleys around Kanajorssuit. Here I think I heard shouts of distress on several occasions, but I could not figure out where the voice was coming from. In the twilight all the kayakmen returned, with the exception of Enok Mathæussen, and late evening came without him having appeared. In spite of this, nobody had any doubts that he would come, being so clever, careful and insightful and able to handle any kind of storm. Besides, the weather had, as previously mentioned, been particularly beautiful today.

Ten o'clock passed without him having arrived. When I came out at four o'clock in the morning the next day, my first stop was the place where his kayak usually lay, and I looked in through his window, but his wife lay there on the bench alone. We immediately sent out people to search the area at Ekallunguit. Lars alone would rather nip out to Simiutat (the group of islands in front of the inlet at the Ameragdlik fjord), and he was the one who found Enok.

There he lay, neatly washed up on a little shingle in the fjord, with his head resting on a little stone and his face turned to the east, exactly as if he might have been arranged by someone. Nobody could understand in what way he might have perished, but people guessed that his oar must have been knocked from his hand while hunting seals, but what then? Why was he so heavily wrapped, both around his face and his wrists, in such weather as there was yesterday?

This incident was, and remained, incomprehensible. He, the generous one, how missed he'd be by both widows and the fatherless! It was he too that had, without a second thought, taken care of Setherak's bereaved the moment he perished. God will bless him according to the word: "Blessed are the merciful, for they shall be shown mercy." I too would come to miss our dear *Parssissok*!

The many hunting sites of the Ameralik fjord would never again see a better person than he was; he loved to go there in particular, but now his life is complete!—As I write, I feel the urge to direct attention to something that I have wanted to reprimand people for doing, namely: the horrible accusation that they far too frequently make of deceased kayakmen whose bodies aren't found. People spread the presumption that they haven't really perished, but have given themselves to fell walking.[20] However, these slanderers know quite well that fell walking is something that people have always been afraid of and that Kivitut today are considered ghosts. They are still not ashamed to say that they have both seen and heard Kivitut, and think nothing of the extent to which they add new sorrow to the one that the victims' bereaved already feel through losing their providers.

Of the two cases where I have been witness to such talk, one concerned a deceased Kangek-ker (from Kangek) and the other a Kangerdlu-arssukker (from Kangerdluarssuk). At Kangek, the wife became practically despairing, since she now had to give up hope of a happy reunion with her husband in the hereafter. The sorrow became joy the next summer as the body of the drowned one was found washed ashore in a little cove, as well as his kayak, which his body still rested in.

Concerning the man from the other place, I have heard his mother complain pitifully over the sorrow her son has brought on her by becoming a Kivitok.

20. *In the days of superstition it was believed that people, who for one reason or another became tired of society, would flee and hide among the fells. Afterwards, they were feared as ghosts or revenants. In Greenland, such people are called Kivitut and are unblessed.*

As if it wasn't enough that the slanderers deceive their fellow people in this unworthy way, they should also consider the extent to which they incur the penalty for lying.

No, let us believe, of the people who perish upon the dangerous seas, that they rest their limbs in the sea bed's great cemetery, and that their souls live in the joy of eternity.

Kayaker launched from land.

A Bear Story
by
J.H.

∎

I finally provide that which, for so long, I have wished to give to the "entertainment periodical." It isn't grand, but it is something I have seen with my own eyes. It concerns certain heathen customs upon catching a bear in southern regions, and which I don't believe are commonly known elsewhere.

It was August 1882-83 down at Augpilagtut in Pamiagdluk. Only two Greenlander houses stand there. In one of them lived three seal hunters along with their family, namely Benjamin, called Akiitit, Isak or Umangujok and Moritz. In the other lived Mathæus, who was mostly called *Uliokakangamik* ("The stuffed full") one, from one of his own adages. The latter was over 70, but still hunted quite regularly. He had also once dealt with a bear single-handedly.

Now for what I wanted to narrate!—It was a Sunday, when the other hunters had gone to sea, and those of us that remained held a prayer in Mathæus' house. Afterwards Benjamin's son, who was the first to leave the house after the service, immediately came charging back in saying that there was a big bear standing right outside the house eating the blubber. I was just as surprised as I was happy to hear this news, whereas old Mathæus was practically quivering with delight, as he exclaimed: "Thanks be he who brings this good news—I must immediately go to stab this bear!" As I looked at him, he stood fumbling. I thought that he was seeking out a really solid tool, a long knife or some such thing, but far from it! The weapon he had equipped himself with barely poked out of his closed hand. What would that do against the hide and thick fat layer of the bear, I thought.

In any case the women of the house would not allow him to get to the bear and stood pulling to hold him back—I helped them with this. The women then all let down the tops of their hair and spread it out, so that the bear might take them for men, and for that reason display more fear and stay away from them. Our heathen forefathers believed bears had human intellect.

Since we were afraid that the bear might consider coming at us through the gut-skin window, I too had to think of a weapon, and for that purpose asked for the axe. They had just lent it to the other house, they said, but at the same moment I spotted an *ullo* (woman's knife), which lay on the table next to the oil lamp, and grabbed it along with a lump of wood from a kayak keel, which I intended to tie to the knife as a shaft. No sooner had I picked up these items than one of the people behind me shouted: "Give them here, I have more strength than you!" This was no other than Mathæus' daughter, the widow. She tore both items from me. Now the lounge clock began to strike eleven, and that poxy bear now looked a lot more voracious.[21] I immediately ran to stop the percussion. In my hurry though, I did the wrong thing—ceasing the racket. I finally came to my senses enough to remove the weights and let the noise continue.

The women still dragged at Mathæus to keep him back. Then, all at once, the mother of he who had reported the bear began to pull her knee-trousers down to her knees (which prevented her free movement) and waddled back and forth across the floor, while plaiting a pair of straws of hay. This, they said, was to weaken the bear's strength. While this went on, old Mathæus got free and dashed out, myself following. I came beside him before he had fully left the entrance passage.[22] He shushed me and said: "Be quiet— now it is going down to the sea."

Mathæus' rifle lay in his kayak, which lay above the beach, and the moment he saw the bear go past it, he sneaked the same way, carefully crawling on all fours. I myself remained standing at the house, and from there saw how the bear suddenly turned to face him, roaring, and was so frightened that I ran over to the other house, where I fell in through the doorway in haste. While I still lay fumbling on the ground,

21. Bears, it is said, are taunted by clanging noises, just as bulls are when they see red.
22. The entrance passage is very long, dark and crooked, so it takes a comparatively long time to get through.

I could see through the window how the bear and Mathæus unflinchingly stared at each other, each from their side of the kayak. Mathæus sneered at the bear, and it roared with its entire mouth open towards him. Now Mathæus placed his food solidly against the kayak and fired. He had not taken his eyes off the bear for a single moment during his preparations.

I now hurried out again and just managed to see him plunge the seal lance into it. Then he shouted towards the house in a loud voice, to say that they were now welcome to come down and get their *ningek* (meat chunks). The summoned women, in their eagerness to get past each other, almost got stuck in the narrow part of the entrance passage, which they accidentally managed to break pieces off of in places. When they reached the bear they all plunged their hands into the open wound and drank blood from it, as each one immediately mentioned the part of the animal that they wanted as their chunk. Then it was my turn to drink from the blood, and I did, as I said that, for my share, I wanted one of the hams. To this, people replied that all limbs were already promised, and that I had neglected to touch the animal the moment I came to the place, invalidating the request. It was a real shame that I had not remembered this fact.

Now the mother of the one who reported the bear ran off to get some water, and when she got back she let all of us take a drink from the cup, though none of us were thirsty. This was, she said, in order to give her son regular bear-luck, and the bit with the blood had been to show the entire bear family their reverence and desire for it. Before they began to flense, they drummed on the bear hide, as they shouted: "You are fat, fat, wonderfully fat!" Which was also done out of politeness, as bears generally tend to be fat, but when we began to open this one, it turned out to be unusually skinny.

Once the head had been brought inside, I followed, since I knew that certain acts were to be carried out with it. The first was it being placed on the edge of the lamp hump *(ipat)* with its face turned towards the southeast, then the eyes and nostrils were stuffed with lamp residue and other similar stuff, while its crown was decorated with all kinds of small things, such as cut boot heels, knives, glass beads, sawdust and other items.

The southeast direction indicates the way from which bears tend to come, namely with the great ice around the southern tip of the country. The moss in its nostrils was to prevent the bear from smelling the approach of humans, and the grease in the mouth was to please it, since it supposedly liked all kinds of burnt fat. They decorate the head with small items, because they think the bear is sent on an errand to them by their forefathers to get these things, and since people believed that the soul of the bear would never make it home until after five days passed, people never ate the head of the bear until this time, as the soul of the bear might die en route and the trinkets for the family would be lost. Also the throat holes (behind the cutoff point of the head) were plugged to prevent exsanguination on the way.

I will without further ado declare all of this idolatry. Our heathen fathers believed that all things, living and dead, had a soul. This should in no way be confused with that of humans, the immortal. The fact that people here, so far to the south, even these days and so long after the introduction of Christianity, can cling to some of the "old" customs, comes from the fact that almost not a year goes by without them coming into contact with the heathens from the east coast.

In 1885 I left Augpilagtut. I cannot really be sure whether there might also be some families out at Pamiagdluk who still held to the bear superstition, but there are not many, and certainly not Isak's. As regards other places, such as this entire colony, people barely know of these strange customs.

The time I was down there, I knew just as little about the day the head was to be cooked as I knew about all other customs. I was completely ignorant about it when it took place, right up until I was given a sudden request to come and eat with them. When we were to begin, I immediately cut off the snout. I was then thoroughly reprimanded, while it was just as quickly torn out of my hand again. I was undeniably quite insulted by this, and told them straight up that I didn't believe a single bit of all this, and they could consider me as foolish as they wanted.

They assured me in all seriousness that I, in that case would never manage to catch a bear. I in turn replied that this would probably turn out to be correct, since I was so short sighted that the bear would be able to lick me before I ever spotted it.

Of other customs there are the following: If they see the tracks of bears in the snow, then they eat a bit of it, to ensure a catch (in the event that the same bear might turn back along the same tracks). Small boys are given the kidneys to eat in order to become strong and brave for bear hunting. They are similarly, for the afore-mentioned five days where the bears soul is trav-eling, careful about producing clanging noises. Mathæus said that the bear I had seen him fell had been his eleventh, and that he had felt no fear of this one, because he had had his rifle available. On a previous occasion—he said—he had suddenly seen one come crawling up over the beach, and he immediately ran at it with only his lance and downed it, just as it was on its way into a group of boulders, but he could not recall how long ago.

The above tale provides an eye catching and twofold interest, as it in addition to being enter-taining and well told, is an unambiguous and in-teresting addendum to the question of the Eski-mos' wanderings and stays among other peoples. Both Indians and Ostyaks used to throw parties upon the downing of a bear and decorate its head, partially to mimic their shamans or miracle men, who during their incantations, dressed themselves in the hide and face of the wolf and the bear, covered it with all kinds of knicknacks, probably because the bear was, on the whole, a worshipped animal. Strangest to me of all is the memory, preserved in the little, secluded Greenlandic community, of the respect for the bear's snout. Castren, among others, says: "The Ostyaks too have a solemn oath pledged over the muzzle of the bear." This applies not only to the Ostyaks but to many other tribes as well.

Note: The narrator J.H. can be none other than the catechist Johannes Hansen, known as Hanserak, who in 1884-85 participated in Captain Gustav Holm's well known umiak expedition to the east coast of Greenland, including wintering at Angmagssalik. Hanserak's diary—a series of supremely interesting records of the wonderful habits and customs of his heathen countrymen—has also been reported in the columns of Atuagagdliutit. ("The Diary of Johannes Hansen" is available from IPI Press.)